CONSUMING
PASSIONS

Dining from Antiquity to the Eighteenth Century

CONSUMING PASSIONS

Dining from Antiquity to the Eighteenth Century

EDITED BY

MAUREEN CARROLL, D.M. HADLEY & HUGH WILLMOTT

TEMPUS

First published 2005

Tempus Publishing Limited
The Mill, Brimscombe Port,
Stroud, Gloucestershire, GL5 2QG
www.tempus-publishing.com

British Library Cataloguing in Publication Data.
A catalogue record for this book is available from the British Library.

ISBN 0 7524 3445 4

Typesetting and origination by Tempus Publishing Limited
Printed in Great Britain

CONTENTS

Illustrations   7

1   Introduction: setting the table
Maureen Carroll, D.M. Hadley and Hugh Willmott   11

DINING IN THE ROMAN WORLD

2   Portraying opulence at the table in Roman Gaul and Germany
Maureen Carroll   23

3   Cooking like a native, dining like a Roman: food preparation
and consumption in Roman Switzerland
Caty Schucany   39

4   Dining *al fresco* with the living and the dead in Roman Italy
Emma-Jayne Graham   49

DINING IN THE MIDDLE AGES

5   Hanseatic table culture in northern Europe 1200-1600: the
archaeology of cultural transfer and resistance
David Gaimster   67

6   Pottery and manners
Duncan Brown   87

7   Dining in disharmony in the later Middle Ages
D.M. Hadley   101

8 Tudor dining: object and image at the table
  Hugh Willmott   121

9 Lunch at the Topkapi Palace: the archaeology of the table during
  Ottoman times
  Joanita Vroom   143

10 Eating *al fresco*: the use of garden buildings for dining in the
  eighteenth-century English pleasure ground
  Kate Felus   163

  Index   183

ILLUSTRATIONS

1 Gravestone of the legionary soldier Titus Iulius Tuttius, c.AD 85-90, Cologne

2 Tables, tablewares and serving wares on funerary reliefs of soldiers and veterans in the first and early second centuries AD

3 Tables, tablewares and serving wares on funerary reliefs of the advanced second and third centuries AD

4 Gravestone of the legionary veteran Gaius Iulius Maternus and his wife, c.AD 160-170, Cologne

5 Grave reliefs showing serving, dining and cooking scenes on the family tomb of the Secundinii at Igel near Trier, c.AD 220-230

6 Grave relief showing a man and a woman reclining, and another woman seated with a child at the table, Bonn, c. AD 200

7 Silver cup (kantharos) from the House of the Menander in Pompeii, late first century BC

8 Grave relief of a family of men and women dining, Mainz (Germany), c.220-230

9 Marble sarcophagus of Publius Caecilius Vallianus in Rome showing servants bringing in food on large platters, third century AD

10 Map showing the location of Aquae Helveticae/Baden (Switzerland)

11 Pottery forms of the late La Tène period (c.100 BC) from central Switzerland (Schweizer Mittelland), and of the third quarter of the first century AD. From Aquae Helveticae/Baden

12 Cooking wares from Italy

13 Aquae Helveticae. Traditions of vessel types I

14 *Aquae Helveticae.* Traditions of vessel types II
15 Wash basins from Italy and Vindonissa
16 Composition of eating vessels in Italy and in *Aquae Helveticae*/Baden
17 Composition of drinking vessels in Italy and in *Aquae Helveticae*/Baden
18 Composition of cooking vessels in Italy and in *Aquae Helveticae*/Baden
19 Garden *biclinium* and pool, Ostia
20 Reconstructed pergola shading diners reclining on a *triclinium*, House of Hercules, Pompeii
21 Vine-covered pergola shading the *triclinium* of the House of Sallust, Pompeii
22 *Triclinium* tomb of Gnaeus Vibrius Saturninus, Pompeii
23 Plan of funerary *triclinium* and well in Tomb 22, Via Laurentina, Ostia
24 *Biclinium* outside Tomb 15, Isola Sacra
25 House tombs with *biclinia*, Isola Sacra
26 Selection of highly decorated red earthenwares and imported German proto- and full stonewares excavated from Kalmar
27 Fire-damaged lead-glazed redware jug from Lihula, Estonia
28 *Jacobakanne* drinking-jugs from Waldenburg, Saxony
29 Stoneware goblets from the Lausitz in Saxony
30 Frechen stoneware *Schnelle* tankard from Malmö
31 Map of the location of Novgorod
32 Plan of medieval Novgorod showing the distribution and relative concentrations of German stoneware and South Baltic redware
33 Pie chart representing the relative quantities by weight of Anglo-Norman vessel types
34 Quantities of vessel types in the Anglo-Norman period from nine sites in Southampton
35 Anglo-Norman pottery
36 Pie chart representing the relative quantities by weight of high medieval vessel types
37 Quantities of vessel types in the high medieval period from nine sites in Southampton
38 Pie chart representing the relative quantities by weight of late medieval vessel types
39 Quantities of vessel types in the late medieval period from nine sites in Southampton
40 Late medieval local pottery
41 Bar chart showing the relative quantities of jar / cooking pots, jugs, bowls and other vessels in late thirteenth-century phases at five different dwellings
42 Servants and musicians attend the royal table
43 Peacock feast

44 Gluttony

45 Puzzle jug from Oxford

46 Puzzle jug from Saintonge (France)

47 A late thirteenth-century copper-alloy aquamanile

48 A fourteenth-century face jug

49 A late thirteenth-century knight jug

50 A medieval fight

51 Schematic representation of the various classes of material culture used in dining

52 Part of the 'Armada Service' parcel-gilt dishes 1581-1601

53 Pewter dish with the ostrich feather of Arthur Prince of Wales, 1485-1503

54 Engraved hunt scene goblet 1577

55 Engraved floral scene 'KY' goblet 1583

56 Engraved tazza, Minster House, London

57 Two engraved goblets from Southampton, 1580s

58 Floral engraved goblets from a) Cheapside, London b) Blomfield Street, London c) Wood Hall, Yorks

59 Detail of cipher on the 'KY' goblet 1583

60 Engraved goblet, IN:GOD:IS:AL:MY:TRVST 1586

61 Portrait of the Dutch ambassador Cornelis Calkoen (1696-1764)

62 Drawing of the Topkapi Palace in Istanbul

63 Painting of ambassador Cornelis Calkoen and his entourage crossing the 2nd courtyard of the Topkapi Palace

64 Painting of ambassador Cornelis Calkoen in audience with Sultan Ahmed III

65 Picture of a so-called *sini* with metal dishes on top

66 Imperial kitchens in the Topkapi Palace

67 Fragments of Iznik Ware, found at excavations in Greece

68 New and old prices of Iznik and Kütahya Wares in a 1600 AD

69 Fragments of Kütahya Ware, found at excavations in Greece

70 The Banqueting House at Gibside (Co. Durham)

71 The elaborate plasterwork of the main room at Horton Menagerie (Northants)

72 The Fishing Room at Kedleston (Derbys)

73 The Octagon Tower at Studley Royal (Yorks)

74 The cave-like kitchen next to the Octagon Tower, Studley Royal (Yorks)

75 Mowbray Point at Hackfall (Yorks)

76 The interior of the Ionic Temple at Rievaulx Terrace (Yorks)

77 The Garden House and Wilderness at Mount Edgcumbe House (Devon)

78 The Grotto at Stowe (Bucks)

COLOUR PLATES

1 Cobalt-blue drinking cup (*kantharos*) imitating a cup of silver, Cologne, first century AD
2 Floor mosaic from the House of the Buffet Supper at Antioch showing silver vessels and food served in them, early third century AD
3 Pottery from the Celtic settlement (*oppidum*) of Basel-Münsterhügel, mid-first century BC
4 Bottles and pear-shaped jars of the early second century AD made in the native tradition from *Aquae Helveticae*/Baden
5 Garden *biclinium* in the House of Loreius Tiburtinus, Pompeii
6 Plan of Tombs 80-77 and their *biclinia*, Isola Sacra
7 *The Holy Family at a Meal* by Jan Mostaert
8 High medieval pottery
9 Late medieval imported pottery
10 Feast of the Duke de Berry
11 A fourteenth-century dining scene
12 Detail taken from 'The life and death of Sir Henry Unton'
13 Maiolica portrait dish, workshop of Cornelis Lubberts, Haarlem 1483
14 Painting of meal given by grand vizier in the Topkapi Palace in honour of ambassador Cornelis Calkoen by Jean-Baptiste Vanmour
15 Ottoman miniature by Levnî, *Surnâme-I Vehbi*, Topkapi Palace Museum Library (fol 50a), 1712 AD
16 Humphry Repton's view of Longleat (Wilts) from Prospect Hill

one

INTRODUCTION: SETTING THE TABLE

Eating and drinking are the most basic requirement for human beings, yet the rituals that surround the preparation, serving and consumption of food and drink reveal that they were complex undertakings of immense social and symbolic importance. Anthropological, archaeological and historical studies have shown how diet, culinary habits and behaviour are influenced by political, cultural and social ideas and relationships between groups of equal or varying status. This introductory chapter provides an overview of the history of dining, beginning with the earliest known evidence for the manufacture of specific dining utensils, through to the earliest evidence for complex dining rituals from ancient Egypt and Greece. This sets the scene for the volume, and is followed by a brief account of the nature of, and evidence for, dining from Antiquity to the eighteenth century.

DINING IN EARLY SOCIETIES

The earliest artefacts used in the consumption of food and drink are many thousands of years old. Evidence for the consumption of shellfish cooked on an open fire by Neanderthals, the predecessors of modern humans, has been found in a cave on the Rock of Gibraltar. Archaeological remains revealed that they used small flint implements for levering their supper out of the shells. At this site there was clearly no separate space for dining – a small child had defecated in the ashes of the fire before the party moved on! Some of the earliest examples of the material culture of dining are also many thousands of years old. For example, a flat wooden artefact from a Palaeolithic (or 'Old Stone Age') site known as Abric Romaní, near Barcelona (Spain) has been tentatively interpreted as the earliest known plate and dates from over 40,000 years ago. A bone implement over 20,000 years old, from what is now the Czech Republic, decorated with a herring-bone pattern has been interpreted as a spoon while a two-pronged implement of similar date and provenance has been labelled as the earliest known fork – although others suggest that it is a representation of a female figure! More convincing evidence survives from the Neolithic period (or 'New Stone Age') when ceramic tablewares are found. These include bowls, jugs, pots and dishes decorated with incised and impressed patterns and burnishing from the Balkans, dating to around 5,000 years ago. Tall-necked amphorae, collared flasks and drinking cups are often found together in tombs in Denmark at around the same date, and these are believed to have been used together for mixing potent drinks and were probably used in a drinking ceremony. What appears to be a Neolithic fruit bowl has been found at Roztoky (Czech Republic). It has been argued that the earliest use of ceramic vessels was a means for groups within these early societies to signal affinity and allegiance.

At the Maszycka Cave, near Cracow (Poland), there is intriguing evidence of the organisation of food preparation by early humans around 15,000 years ago. In a rear chamber of the cave system were the butchered bones of many large animals, and it has been suggested that this was an area in which cuts of meat were stored – perhaps the earliest-known example of a walk-in fridge! Some of the earliest cave art typically includes depictions of the animals eaten by the communities that created the art, and at the Cuervas de la Araña, Bicorp (Spain) a woman is depicted collecting honey in a jar – are these mankind's first menus?

THE EARLIEST EVIDENCE FOR COMPLEX DINING RITUALS

The earliest societies from which a range of archaeological, written and pictorial evidence survives permit much greater understanding of the rituals surrounding, and the social significance of, dining. From the third millennium BC in Egypt the walls of the tombs of nobles and high-ranking officials were decorated with colourful paintings depicting scenes of the preparation and serving of food and drink, often in the presence of, and being set before, the deceased who symbolically, even in death, lived a good life of culinary opulence. Some of the most extensive and well preserved paintings in this regard were found in the tomb of Nakht, a noble of the early fourteenth century BC, near Thebes.

Characteristic of such scenes are the display of tables laden with food, including bread, cakes, grapes, figs, lettuces, leeks, pomegranates and gourds, as well as cuts of meat, fish and game birds. The preparation of food includes not only the butchering of animals, the plucking of geese and ducks, the processing of wheat and the making of bread, but also the pressing of grapes and the bottling of their juice in earthenware containers. Foodstuffs are served in large ceramic and metal bowls and platters and in baskets, whilst drink, both beer and wine, is brought in by servants carrying cups, goblets and flasks. In addition to the pictures of food, different kinds of poultry, meat, bread, figs and dried fish were deposited in plates and baskets in the tombs to provide the deceased with what would be needed for life after death.

In the wall paintings the recipients of these culinary delights, however, are generally depicted as observers of the activities around them rather than as actual consumers of the meals. Clearly the array of food and the large entourage of personnel necessary for the provision, preparation and serving of food and drink visually signalled the privileged position, power and wealth of the recipients.

In the ancient Near East opulent banquets at which food and drink was consumed are focused on court rituals surrounding the royal family. One of the stone reliefs from the palace at Ninevah in Assyria dating to about 650 BC shows the king Ashurbanipal reclining on a couch under a vine trellis in his garden, whilst the queen sits in a chair at his feet. Both drink from cups taken from a table at the side of the couch. They are attended by several servants in the king's command who bear platters of food, cool the royal couple in the hot Assyrian climate by waving fans above their heads, and also make music. Here we have an early depiction of opulent dining *al fresco*!

The earliest dining scenes in the ancient Greek world, dating to the Late Bronze Age (ca. 1550-1100 BC), appear in frescoes adorning the walls of the palaces at Knossos in Minoan Crete and Pylos in Mycenaean Greece. Although the hunting of game and the preparation of food and drink for a feast are depicted in these frescoes, the only commodity shown in the process of actually being consumed is wine, as witnessed by men who are seated on stools or chairs at a table and who hold a drinking cup. In fact, the importance of drinking rituals, and perhaps competitive drinking, amongst the wealthy elite of Mycenaean society on the Greek mainland is attested by the deposition in grand built tombs of exotic cups and jugs of gold, silver and bronze that were imported from Crete and the Cyclades in the eastern Mediterranean. In the *Iliad* and the *Odyssey*, the Homeric epics describing Late Bronze Age society (but recorded as late as 700 BC), wine drinking was considered a particularly manly and heroic activity.

Drinking scenes are a prevalent feature of Greek art from about 600 BC, particularly in the scenes painted on ceramic cups and bowls used for drinking wine. These scenes take up the oriental motif of individuals of elevated social status reclining to eat and drink that we have already encountered in Assyria in the seventh century. To recline whilst drinking and eating in specially designed dining rooms in the house, and being waited on by servants, had become a sign of prestige and power. Since the painted drinking vessels depict activities surrounding the symposion, the upper-class drinking party conducted after the meal to which only men were invited, the women shown participating in such social gatherings are limited to hired dancing girls, flute girls, prostitutes and high-class courtesans, but never include the respectable wives of the host and his guests. More sober banquets are represented on Greek funerary monuments, especially in the second and first centuries BC in the eastern Mediterranean. These are often attended by men, their wives and children in the company of servants ready to serve drinks and meals and to clear away cups and plates. Such scenes are meant to represent an idealised situation of private life, but the reclining figures also represent the deceased in an heroic pose and as subjects of religious veneration. Nevertheless, even here there is much more emphasis on the consumption of wine and the rituals conducted to prepare and serve it than on the actual food served during the meal.

Probably through cultural and economic contact with the Greeks, this custom spread to Italy where it was adopted by the Etruscans. Our best source of information on Etruscan dining habits are the paintings and reliefs adorning the walls of chamber tombs in Etruria (today Tuscany) from the sixth century BC. Some of these, such as the scenes in the early fifth-century Tomb of the Diver in Paestum, reflect the custom of the Greek male drinking party, depicting only men engaged in drinking wine and taking part in drinking games. Others, such as the early fifth-century wall paintings in the Tomb of the Leopards at Tarquinia, however, show mixed sex dining, with families of women and men reclining at an event that involved more than just drinking wine. Servants and musicians are present to serve and entertain the guests. Also deposited in these tombs are painted drinking vessels and large bowls for mixing water and wine imported from Greece, and primarily from Athens, indicating that the material culture of drinking in the Greek style had been adopted by Etruscan nobles.

DINING IN ROMAN SOCIETY

We are well informed about Roman dining culture through a wide variety of media, particularly from the first century BC. As Katherine Dunbabin has demonstrated, banquets are described in contemporary written sources and are depicted in Roman art, and the material culture of Roman dining survives in the form of cups, platters and bowls made of precious metals, rock crystal and glass, and above all in pottery. The latter can be studied to reveal different combinations of Roman and native cooking and dining implements in various parts of the Roman world outside Italy. Moreover, precious examples of furniture such as dining tables, serving tables and dining couches made of wood, sometimes decorated with ivory carvings, and bronze survive. Late Roman tapestries and hangings that once adorned dining rooms are preserved in Egypt.

Possibly since the sixth century BC aristocratic Romans, in emulation of the Greeks, reclined to dine, although literary sources indicate that it was far more common in early Roman history to be seated at the meal. Dining throughout the Roman world was not necessarily a male affair, and there was a greater focus on the display and consumption of food. As contemporary sources tell us, formal dining for both sexes in the company of each other, and in the company of children and youths, was common. All sorts of entertainment were provided. At banquets in the dining rooms and gardens in the homes and villas of upper-class Romans, social bonds and obligations between the host and his guests were forged and cemented. Moreover, the really wealthy aristocrats and aspiring politicians often displayed generosity in very public ways, staging large banquets with free food and drink to which numerous, but probably selected, members of the public were invited. Julius Caesar, for example, hosted banquets in Rome after his military triumphs in 45 BC at which participants placed on 22,000 dining couches were fed. Such displays of public benefaction were designed to impress and win favour with one's fellow citizens and peers. Our sources on Roman dining therefore are very informative on social competition and on notions of hospitality and etiquette. Less formal dining in the form of picnics took place outdoors, as Roman mosaics and wall paintings indicate. Aristocratic and luxurious dining is a prevalent feature of Roman funerary art, and banquets were conducted at the tomb itself in the festivals held to celebrate rituals associated with the cult of the dead.

EARLY MEDIEVAL DINING

During the first centuries after the fall of the Roman Empire, the so-called 'Dark Ages', the range of available evidence for dining is comparatively limited. Nonetheless, it is possible to discern that eating and drinking was an important constituent part of both religious and secular society in the early medieval period, but that it often posed a social, moral or religious conundrum. The feast hall played an extremely important role in royal and aristocratic society in Anglo-Saxon England, and the feasts that took place in such halls are frequently referred to in Anglo-Saxon literature. In her recent study of Anglo-Saxon feast halls, Marjorie Brown has highlighted that these halls were a place where lords displayed to their fellow lords and their retainers their status. This was achieved through the quantity and quality of the food and drink on offer, and through associated festivities and rituals such as gift-giving. We might note, for example, that the legendary hero Beowulf was rewarded for killing the monster Grendel in the king's feast hall with lavish gifts, including a sword, helmet and horses with jewelled saddles. The feast hall was a place in which social bonds were both made and reinforced. In the Old English poem *The Battle of Maldon*, which recounts events during an assault by a Viking army in 991, one of the warriors urged on his comrades with the words 'let us call to mind those declarations we often uttered over mead, when from our seat we heroes in hall would put up brave pledges about tough fighting'. Conversely, feast halls could also be dangerous places, in which consumption of too much alcohol might lead to violence. For example, in the Old English poem *Judith*, derived from the Old Testament book of this name, the Assyrian King Holofernes drank to excess during a feast: 'He laughed and bawled and roared and made a racket so that the children of men could hear from far away how the stern-minded man bellowed and yelled, insolent and crazed with mead'. Yet, despite the prominent position of feast in Anglo-Saxon literature archaeological evidence for the nature of these halls is scarce. Perhaps the most well-known examples of a royal hall were excavated at Yeavering (Northumberland) in the 1950s, where a series of wooden halls were found, the largest measuring 25m by 12m. The site appears to date to the sixth or seventh century, but unfortunately few artefacts were recovered to illuminate the nature of the activities that took place here. That it is likely to have been a gathering place for many is indicated by the discovery of an adjacent wooden 'amphitheatre' with a stage and raised seats. The recent excavation of a richly furnished 'princely' grave at Prittlewell (Essex) may throw some light on the material culture of Anglo-Saxon feasting, as the grave goods included a bronze flagon and bowl, probably from the Mediterranean, and decorated wooden drinking vessels.

Within religious circles, dining presented potential problems. The consumption of ritual meals associated with worship of pagan deities was condemned by Christian commentators, and early medieval hagiographical accounts describe the response of ecclesiastics to such behaviour. For example, when the sixth-century saint Columbanus came across a group of Alemanns making an offering of ale to the pagan god Woden, he blew on the cask of ale causing it to split open and spill its contents. A fear that new converts to Christianity might revert back to pagan behaviour and rituals meant that feasting could be a contentious issue, especially if non-Christian ritual components were detected. Although, as Bonnie

Effros has recently observed, some clerical condemnations were stereotypical and influenced by depictions of pagan behaviour in the late Antique world, there was clearly a contemporary concern in sixth- and seventh-century Frankia about the subversive qualities of feasting and its associated revelries. Excessive feasting by clerics was not unknown, and was condemned. A seventh-century account of an Easter feast hosted by the Bishop of Issoire provided a warning of the dangers of clerical excess, when a group of priests began to mock fellow priests who were doing penance – the collapse of the house in which the feast was held left only the bishop and the penitents alive. The holy were inclined to be abstemious when it came to the consumption of food and drink, and occasional fasting was common. For example, the English saint Æthelthryth only ate one meal a day, while her contemporary St Wilfrid was recorded by his biographer as never finishing off a whole glass while dining. Extreme fasting was another response to food among early medieval ecclesiastics, and while liable to be condemned such ascetic behaviour provided a means for some, especially women, to enhance their status.

Feasting remained, nonetheless, an important component of Christian life, and saints were inclined to reward the faithful with abundant food and drink, although there was concern that this was not taken to excess. As Effros has recently argued, the Christian community was partly defined through the consumption of food and drink at Eucharistic, funerary and familial meals. Meals associated with funerals are poorly documented, but are elucidated by archaeological remains, although it is not always easy to distinguish the remains of feasting from food offerings, nor to be certain that the connotations were entirely Christian. For example, excavations at Réville (France) revealed vessels, animal bones and marine shellfish in many seventh-century burials, while eggs, chicken, cuts of meat, sage, mustard, beer and wine had been deposited in fifth-century burials at Cologne (Germany). The exclusion of some individuals from dining with Christians was a means to ensure their identification as outsiders. For example, the Council of Agde (506) instructed Christians not to dine with Jews or heretics or face excommunication, while Gregory of Tours cited dining with Arians as a threat to Catholic stability.

LATE MEDIEVAL AND POST–MEDIEVAL EUROPE

From the thirteenth century onwards there are a greater number of sources that shed light on the nature of dining in Europe. However, the majority of these inevitably focus on elite groups. Reconstructing the diet and dining patterns of peasants and the lower orders of societies is more difficult, but both historical and archaeological sources do provide some clues. One of the best-known medieval texts describing the life of a peasant is William Langland's *Piers the Plowman*, written during the late fourteenth century. What is interesting is that it indicates that at least some peasants could have a surprisingly varied diet. Piers' cottage was described as containing foodstuffs such as cheese, curd and cream as well as oats, bran and beans. Most of those living in the country, and probably many in the towns, would have supplemented their diets with home-grown vegetables, and meat would have been available at certain times of the year either cured or fresh, as most households owned at least one pig.

The types of dishes that peasants dined on are also sometimes mentioned in texts or even illustrated in documents. Breads made from barley and oats formed the staple of most people's diets, but these would have been supplemented with pottages, soups and porridges. Fermented ales also played an important nutritional role as well as being a safe liquid to drink. The relatively simple nature of these dishes did not require particularly complex material culture for their consumption. However, the common misapprehension that peasants did not possess many personal goods, especially not those associated with dining, probably develops from the lack of surviving remains. Wooden bowls and dishes would have been common items in any household, and in the rare instances where survival conditions are rather better, such as at the medieval town of Novgorod in Russia, discussed in this volume by David Gaimster, wooden artefacts are found in large numbers even in the poorest contexts. Similarly most drinking vessels would have been made from perishable items such as horn and leather and simply do not survive to the present day. Also problematic is that even items that might be expected to survive archaeologically, such as ceramic cooking pots, are often absent on settlement sites. This is not to say that such wares were not being used, indeed the number of keys and lock fittings found at a number of medieval villages suggests that people had belongings that they were actively protecting. The explanation lies in the fact that, contrary to many popular images, medieval peasants kept their houses spotlessly clean and any breakages were swept up and deposited along with the general household waste on the surrounding fields.

Poorer people living in the towns probably had a different experience of dining. Whilst food was still consumed at home using simple vessels that would have been familiar to the rural dweller, the urban environment provided a great variety of eating locations. Large towns around northern Europe, such as London, Paris or Nuremberg, all had a variety of markets, often specialising in different types of goods. While many sold unprepared foodstuffs, it is clear that street stalls where the passer-by could purchase hot soups, pies or sausages were almost always present. A recent study by Martha Carlin of street vending in

London has shown that such 'fast' food, far from being for the wealthy, catered primarily to the poorest groups of society who otherwise might not have been able to purchase and cook such foods for themselves. Some contemporary illustrations, such as those in the early fifteenth-century *Concilium Constantiense* from Constance in Germany, also show that to make their wares even more available, vendors sold food from carts drawn through the street, which the pedestrian could stop as required.

The urban dweller would also have had the opportunity to visit a variety of alehouses, premises that did not spread outside the confines of the town until the sixteenth and seventeenth centuries. The earliest recorded of these seem to date from the late twelfth century, when they may have consisted of no more than a counter at the door of a private house. However, during the later medieval period and in the larger European towns, alehouses did become larger, having seating areas, and by the sixteenth century it was not uncommon for cheap stews and soups to be available for purchase.

Inevitably a far wider range of sources on dining survives for the richer sections of society. Household accounts provide insights into not only the quantity and range of foodstuffs consumed, but also the incredible organisation involved in organising a meal and ensuring its smooth running. One of the most famous of these still surviving belonged to Alice de Bryene of Acton Hall in Suffolk, and it has recently been re-examined by Ffiona Swabey. Kept for a year between Michaelmas 1412 and Michaelmas 1413, the household account reveals that Dame Alice served more than 16,500 meals to her guests, and most were planned with meticulous care. Guest lists and seating arrangements were carefully considered so that proper hierarchies between diners were observed. Also revealing is that Dame Alice clearly used the meal for an opportunity to conduct business as well; tenants were invited to discuss leases and visiting churchmen to pass on information and gossip about the wider world.

Found alongside the increased number of household accounts and inventories, are educational manuals and treatise giving precise instruction on suitable behaviour at the table. One of the earliest of these, *Disciplina Clericalis*, was written shortly before 1110 by Petrus Alphonsi, a Spanish Jew who converted to Christianity. In this he emphasised the importance of good manners during dining and gave examples of how to behave at the table. From this time onwards, initially in southern Europe but latterly in northern kingdoms, similar texts, such as the late fifteenth-century *Babees Book* in England, reiterate time after time the appropriate ways that the guest was expected to behave. By the early sixteenth century the adoption of the printing press meant that these could be mass-produced and they reached new audiences. Baldassare Castiglione's *Corteziania* and Erasmus of Rotterdam's *de Civilitate Morum Puerilum*, published in 1528 and

1530 respectively, became some of the first books that in modern terms would be described as international best sellers. Good manners and knowing how to behave at the table had become established necessities not only for the richest but also the emerging middle classes.

Coinciding with the widening interest in a regulated system of dining came the increasingly sophisticated paraphernalia found on the table. There was a gradually increasing number of bowls, plates, cups and goblets from the fourteenth century onwards, which finally culminated in the eighteenth century with a situation, still familiar today, in which each diner might expect an individual full set of matching tableware. Not only were numbers of vessels increasing, the materials they were made from were becoming more diverse. Throughout this later period new ceramic types, such as tinglazes, stonewares and creamwares developed, all catering to an increasingly sophisticated consumer taste.

By the early eighteenth century other new trends were developing. The Enlightenment saw the renewed interest in the natural world that was to affect many aspects of daily life for the richer members of society. This was most clearly manifested in the creation of parks, gardens and designed landscapes, and these more often than not included spaces for entertainment and dining in the form of summerhouses, grottoes and follies. Hand in hand with this went an interest in the exotic. Europeans were increasingly in contact with other cultures, and it is no surprise that this affected the way fashionable architecture developed. One of the most famous examples was the Chinese pagoda built at the Kew estate of Princess Augusta, the Dowager Princess of Wales and mother of George III. Designed and built by Sir William Chambers in 1762, it originally formed part of a wider leisure landscape that included a Turkish mosque and an Arabian Alhambra, all features part of a wider leisure landscape with spaces from promenading and dining. As the Romans had over a millennium and a half before them, the eighteenth-century aristocrat was able to dine al fresco and admire the unusual.

CONCLUSION

The focus of this book is the social practice of dining in the historical periods in Europe, roughly the Roman period to the eighteenth century. It examines the archaeological, documentary, material culture and art historical evidence for the consumption of food and drink in various historical, social and cultural contexts. The various chapters in this volume examine a wide variety of aspects of dining. These include the locations in which dining took place, including rooms specifically assigned for dining, gardens, and even cemeteries where feasts to commemorate the dead might be held. Other aspects of the setting for dining considered include furniture, table ware, table decorations and the decoration of dining rooms. The rituals surrounding dining in a variety of periods are examined, including food preparation and presentation, the serving of food and drink, the stages by which they were consumed and the behaviour that was considered appropriate in a wide variety of social and cultural contexts.

Maureen Carroll, D.M. Hadley and Hugh Willmott

ACKNOWLEDGEMENTS

We would like to thank Dr Paul Pettitt for guiding us through the evidence for dining within early human societies. We are also grateful to the British Academy for funding a conference held at the University of Sheffield, at which most of the chapters in this volume were delivered, and Professor Christopher Dyer who supported the application.

BIBLIOGRAPHY

Brown, M., 'The feast hall in Anglo-Saxon society', in M. Carlin and J. Rosenthal (eds), *Food and Eating in Medieval Europe* (London, 1998), pp.1–13

Carlin, M., 'Fast food and urban living standards in medieval England', in M. Carlin and J. Rosenthal (eds), *Food and Eating in Medieval Europe* (London, 1998), pp.27–51

Dunbabin, K., *The Roman Banquet: images of conviviality* (Cambridge, 2003)

Effros, B., *Creating Community with Food and Drink in Merovingian Gaul* (New York, 2002)

Swabey, F., *Medieval Gentlewoman. Life in a widow's household in the later Middle Ages* (Stroud, 1999)

two

PORTRAYING OPULENCE AT THE TABLE IN ROMAN GAUL AND GERMANY

Information on drinking, dining and table practices in Roman Gaul and Germany can be gleaned from an examination of scenes depicting such activities on funerary monuments. These range in date from the last third of the first century to the mid-third century AD, and they are concentrated largely along the Rhine in the two German provinces of Upper and Lower Germany and in the Moselle valley in the province of Belgic Gaul. The reliefs depict individuals and groups using various tablewares and containers at the table, as well as slaves and staff serving and clearing away drinks and meals, and a variety of room furnishings. But is this a realistic rendering of contemporary practice and artefacts in the northwest provinces, or do these scenes depict an ideal situation? In order to answer this, it is necessary to explore the cultural context and social meaning of these images. Furthermore, an examination of surviving vessels in metal, glass and pottery of the same periods is essential to determine what those vessels on the funerary reliefs represent and whether they reflect a particular selection from the range of contemporary material culture available as a means of displaying status. Finally, the reliefs allow us to explore changes in dining furniture, spatial arrangements at the table, and issues of gender and age of the participants from the early to the late Roman period in the region.

SOLDIERS, ALCOHOL AND THE 'GOOD LIFE'

The earliest funerary monuments to shed light on drinking and dining date to the period from about AD 70 to the early second century, and they originate

1 Gravestone of the legionary soldier Titus Iulius Tuttius, *c.*AD 85-90, Cologne

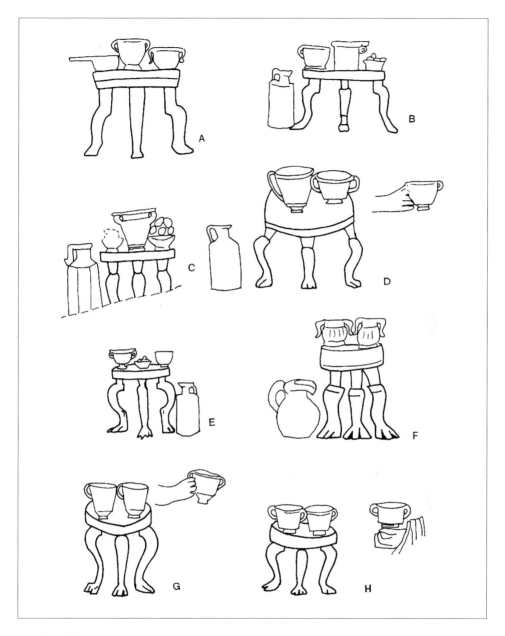

2 Tables, tablewares and serving wares on funerary reliefs of soldiers and veterans in the first and early second centuries AD. A: Gravestone of Silius, soldier in the *Ala Picentiana*, c.AD 70-80, Mainz; B: Gravestone of Mansuetas, soldier in the *Cohors III Lusitanorum*, c.AD 85-90, Cologne; C: Gravestone of a soldier (name not preserved), c.AD 115-120, Bonn; D: Gravestone of Titus Iulius Tuttius, soldier in *Legio XXII Primigenia*, c.AD 85-90, Cologne; E: Gravestone of Marcus Valerius Celerinus, veteran of *Legio X Gemina Pia Fidelis*, and his wife Marcia Procula, c.AD 100, Cologne; F:Gravestone of Iulius Ingenius, soldier in the *Ala I Flavia*, c.AD 70-80, Mainz; G: Gravestone of Gaius Iulius Baccus, soldier in the *Cohors I Thracum*, c.AD 85-90, Cologne; H: Gravestone of Marcus Aemilius Durises, soldier in the *Ala Sulpicia*, c.AD 85-90, Cologne

from various sites along the upper and lower Rhine, from Switzerland to the Netherlands. They are a very uniform group, both in their iconography and in the sector of society they commemorate. They all belonged to soldiers actively serving in the legions and in auxiliary units or to army veterans (*1*). All of them depict the deceased man in an heroic pose reclining on a couch padded with a mattress and holding a cup or chalice of wine in one hand and a napkin in the other. In front of the couch is a small, round table on which stand drinking vessels and the occasional small bowl containing small bits of food (*2*). Next to the table is either a cylindrical or prismatic container for wine, and one or two small male servants or slaves stand in attendance at one end or at either end of the couch. In death, the soldiers commemorated with such monuments could achieve status and standing through an idealised picture of pampered, aristocratic activity.

This type of figural scene is generally known in archaeological literature as a *Totenmahl*, or funerary banquet, and it ultimately derives from eastern Greek funerary reliefs of the second and first centuries BC depicting a ritual meal in honour of the heroised dead. However, the term *Totenmahl* is a bit of a misnomer, since the deceased on the Roman reliefs is always shown drinking, but never actually eating anything. Once Roman soldiers, Italian immigrants and civilians from Romanised parts of Gaul had introduced a variety of different types of gravestones to the German frontier zone in the early first century AD, the funerary banquet monuments suddenly became popular there in the last third of that century. They were used by men who had been recruited in Spain, Gaul, the Alpine regions, Thrace, and the Netherlands.

FAMILY DINING

The *Totenmahl* reliefs ceased to be used by military personnel on the Rhine in the early second century, although they continued to be used by soldiers and civilians (including women) in Britain into the third century, and they were relatively commonly used elsewhere at this late date for soldiers of the imperial equestrian guard. On the Rhine and Moselle, the earlier *Totenmahl* scenes involving male drinking were subsequently adopted by the civilian population for both gravestones and built tombs, mainly around Trier, Neumagen and Arlon, and more rarely in Mainz and Bonn, but notable changes in the number and sex of the participants, in the spatial arrangements at the table, and in the vessels and dining furniture are apparent in these scenes (*3*). The gravestone of the legionary veteran, Gaius Iulius Maternus, dating to shortly after the mid-second century, is one of the earliest signalling these changes (*4*). On this stone in Cologne, Maternus reclines on the couch, and his wife is seated in a wicker chair at the

D·M·C·IVL·MATERNVS
VET·EX·LEG·I·M·VIVS·SIBI
T·MARIE·MARCELLINAE
COIIVGI·DVLCISSIME·
CASTISSIM·OBITAE·F

3 Tables, tablewares and serving wares on funerary reliefs of the advanced second and third centuries AD. A: Gravestone of Gaius Iulius Maternus, veteran of *Legio I Minervia*, and his wife Maria Marcellina, *c.*AD 160-170, Cologne; B: Gravestone of Libera, *c.*AD 170-180, Cologne; C: Gravestone of an unknown family, *c.*AD 180-185, Neumagen; D: Gravestone of an unknown family, end second century AD, Bonn; E: Grave relief of an unknown family, *c.*AD 200, Arlon; F: Grave relief of an unknown family, *c.*AD 220-230, Mainz; G: Grave relief of an unknown family, *c.*AD 220-230, Neumagen; H: Grave reliefs of Lucius Secundinius Securus, Lucius Secundinius Aventinus and family, *c.*AD 250, Igel; I: Grave relief of an unknown family, *c.*AD 220-230, Neumagen

4 Gravestone of the legionary veteran Gaius Iulius Maternus and his wife, *c.*AD 160-170, Cologne

foot of it. The small round table is still there, but now for the first time it has a tablecloth on it, and the emphasis is on food, rather than drink. An enormous platter filled with fruit takes up most of the table surface.

By the late second century, such scenes are enriched with figures of servants bringing in platters of food, and several diners are depicted sitting, or reclining, or combinations of the two, at the table (5). According to Roman literary sources, in the early Republican period women sat at dinner, but by the Empire from the late first century BC the custom was for both sexes to recline when dining formally. Before reaching adulthood, children sat at the foot end of the couches or even at a separate table, but young men gained the right to recline at dinner at about the age of 16. In the dining scenes of the late second and third century in Gaul it is generally the women who sit in chairs, whilst the men recline. But

5 Grave reliefs showing serving, dining and cooking scenes on the family tomb of the Secundinii at Igel near Trier, c.AD 220-230

there are depictions of both men and women sitting, as well as both reclining (6). Perhaps the allocation of a place at the table, and the custom of reclining or sitting, based on sex or age, had begun to change or relax by this time. It is possible that the divergence from traditional Roman habits at the table in Gaul is rooted in family social structures, hierarchies and gender roles that differed from those in Rome and Italy. It is noticeable in this context that many of the Gallic families on these late reliefs wear their local Gallic cloaks and tunics, rather than distinctly 'mainstream' Roman attire. There may not have been one single custom regarding body position at the table that was consistently adhered to everywhere, for there are scenes of formal dining in the late fourth century in North African mosaics where all the men sit at large rectangular tables, whilst as late as the sixth century Gregory of Tours describes a dinner party at which the men reclined, but the host's wife sat in a chair. At any rate, the inclusion of women, and even small children, in these scenes clearly shows that these are meals in a family context. Given the importance of dining as a competitive activity and a display of status, as well as the increasing prominence of the dining room in later Roman domestic architecture, the reliefs also may allude to banquets at which social relationships of power and influence were played out between the host and invited guests.

Possibly to accommodate larger numbers of diners, and large platters of food, the shape and size of the tables change from small and round to rectangular. Round tables still are in use, but they appear to be larger, or taller, than the first-century examples, and many of them are clearly folding tables (3). Tablecloths, some quite woolly in appearance, cover all the tables on the second- and third-century dining scenes. Occasionally, a monopod table or sideboard supporting all manner of drinking paraphernalia is shown in the background or to one side of the dining room, from which servants fetch drinks for the diners. On a few

6 Grave relief showing a man and a woman reclining, and another woman seated with a child at the table, Bonn, c.AD 200

rare monuments, scenes of kitchen activities leading up to and after the meal are represented. The scenes on the mid-third century tomb of the clothiers, Lucius Secundinius Securus and Lucius Secundinius Aventinus, at Igel near Trier are the closest we get to the literary descriptions of banquets involving culinary specialists, cooks, carvers of game birds, and wine waiters (5).

Unlike the first-century *Totenmahl* stones, there is nothing overtly heroic about these dining scenes; rather they have an intimate domestic flavour. They represent formal dining of an opulent nature. Such scenes are characteristic of the large built tombs of the Moselle valley covered in relief panels depicting images of the domestic and working life of the wealthy merchants in the region, scenes such as the sale and inspection of textiles, the transport by river or by road of produce from the estates, and the lady of the house being attended by servants. The size and form of the monuments, but especially the pictorial scenes on them, are designed to advertise the affluence and commercial success of the families they commemorate. Such families engaged in trade and commerce invested in and owned large estates, and, as we can see on some of the reliefs, they had tenant farmers at their disposal who supplied them with all manner of produce. Chickens, fish, pigs, lambs, hares and fruit – all of which will later end up on the dining table – are brought to the estate supervisor on one of the panels on the Igel monument. But, as John Drinkwater has demonstrated, this class of society was not made up of the old aristocratic families of the first century AD, rather they represent the hardworking and successful bourgeoisie. It would be natural for them to emulate aristocratic dining and to add this motif to the catalogue of scenes of daily life on their funerary monuments.

MATERIAL CULTURE: FUNERARY ART *CONTRA* THE ARCHAEOLOGICAL RECORD?

Before considering whether the vessels for eating and drinking shown on the tables reflect what was actually available, archaeological and literary evidence for the tables themselves should be examined. Table legs and other parts of circular wooden tables like those represented on the reliefs occasionally survive in the archaeological record in northwest Europe in contexts dating to the late first century BC. According to contemporary literary sources, desirable sorts of wood for tables were maple and citrus wood from North African Mauretania. Small circular tables with folding legs made of bronze and even silver have also survived. These range in date from the first century BC to the early fourth century AD, and they are usually between 75cm and 1m in height. Many of them appear to be of Italian or Egyptian manufacture, although by the second and third centuries they were also produced in Gaul and Germany. Rectangular, four-legged folding tables made of bronze have also been retrieved from archaeological sites. Like the circular tables, they stood up to a metre in height and were manufactured between the first century BC and the early fourth century AD.

7 Silver cup (*kantharos*) from the House of the Menander in Pompeii, late first century BC

Do the vessels on the funerary reliefs of the first to third centuries correspond to the actual surviving material culture of the region, and, if they do, do they reflect a particular selection from the range of contemporary material available as a means of displaying actual or projected social status? Almost all of the cups on the first-century reliefs are two-handled vessels – *skyphoi* and *kantharoi* – with a stemmed foot or ring base (*2*). They correspond to precious and expensive drinking vessels of these forms in silver, known at a variety of sites in Italy, including Pompeii and Boscoreale (*7*). Such vessels were imitated in glass, lead-glazed pottery and even rock crystal, both the silver cups and their imitations having been produced in Italy and exported to northwest Europe (*colour plate 1*). In Book 33 of his *Natural History*, Pliny says that army officers took silver plate drinking and dining services with them on campaign, and the discovery of Roman silver hoards of the late first century BC east of the Rhine in Germanic territory might be a confirmation of this practice.

In the first-century relief scenes, a crater for mixing water and wine, or a long-handled wine strainer occasionally stands on the table. These too are known in silver and bronze. On the dining room floor next to the table are individual containers, the most commonly represented being a tall, cylindrical or prismatic container with one handle. There can be no doubt that these are glass bottles, of which numerous examples of the first and second centuries, primarily produced in the glass workshops of Cologne, survive. Their purpose is surely to provide the wine used at the table. At Trimalchio's banquet, as portrayed in the first century AD in the *Satyricon* by Petronius, glass jars containing high-quality Falernian wine with labels attached to them were brought into the dining room.

From the middle of the second century, a different range of dishes, cups and other vessels appears on the funerary reliefs. The cups held by men or women are simple hemispherical cups or conical beakers, examples of which are known in silver, but more commonly in glass, in contemporary material culture (*8*). Vessels used in serving drink are the square glass bottles with one handle produced mainly in Cologne in the second and third centuries. On funerary reliefs of the early third century these square bottles (with a ladle?) are sometimes shown stored in a box near the table or kept in a tight-fitting basket. Tall cylindrical glass bottles were also used at the table, and they are sometimes depicted as being wrapped in rope or put in a basket to protect them from damage, and perhaps to keep the liquid in them cool. Servants preparing and pouring drinks at the ancillary monopod table in the dining room use jugs, pitchers and strainers, many of which survive in the archaeological record in silver, bronze and glass, and sometimes in earthenware with a surface coating of mica dust to give the vessels a metallic lustre.

Since the emphasis on the second- and third-century reliefs is far less on drinking, and far more on the display and consumption of food, it is worth looking at the platters displayed on them. The round and oval platters are large, and they take up almost the entire space provided on the round tables. The round tables generally had a diameter of 1m at the very most, and the platters on them are not much smaller than that. The platters on the rectangular tables also are of large dimensions. Large round platters are being taken from the dining room and apparently wiped or washed clean in one part of the dining room and in the kitchen on the Igel monument (*5*). Although the normal diameter of silver dishes may have been about 25cm, round platters in silver over 50cm in diameter, and oval platters in silver and bronze up to 51cm survive at third- and fourth-century sites on the Rhine, in the Ardennes and in Bavaria. Large glass platters increase in number in the first half of the fourth century, possibly to take the place of expensive metal dishes. Either silver or glass could have been used for the platters shown on the reliefs, but silver would have been the most prestigious of the two. Oval platters with ornate flat handles on either end also were produced in glossy red samian ware, in imitation of the metal platters with the same features, but they are never this large, nor do they appear after the first century. The very

1 Cobalt-blue drinking cup (*kantharos*) imitating a cup of silver, Cologne, first century AD

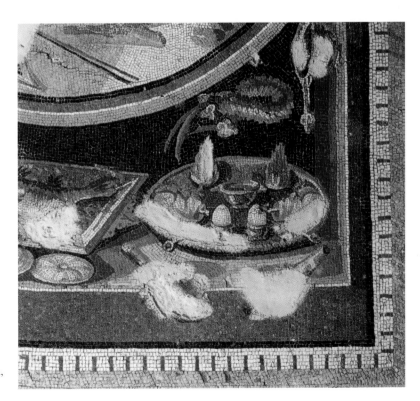

2 Floor mosaic from the House of the Buffet Supper at Antioch showing silver vessels and food served in them, early third century AD

3 Pottery from the Celtic settlement (*oppidum*) of Basel-Münsterhügel, mid-first century BC

4 Bottles and pear-shaped jars of the early second century AD made in the native tradition from *Aquae Helveticae*/Baden

5   Garden *biclinium* in the House of Loreius Tiburtinus, Pompeii

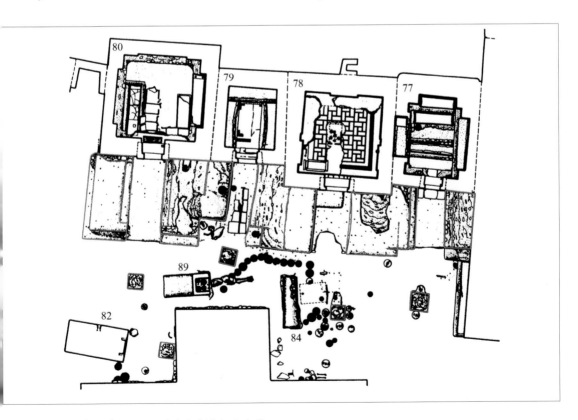

6   Plan of Tombs 80-77 and their *biclinia*, Isola Sacra

Left: 7 The iconic Hanseatic merchant table as depicted in *The Holy Family at a Meal* by Jan Mostaert (*c.*1495-1500). The setting contains a Siegburg stoneware mug and a drinking bowl of the period alongside tableware in other media

Below: 8 High medieval pottery. 1: Southampton coarseware jar/cooking pot; 2: local glazed sandy ware bowl; 3: Saintonge gritty ware mortar; 4: Dorset whiteware jug; 5: Saintonge green-glazed whiteware jug; 6: local redware baluster jug; 7: West Sussex green-glazed jug; 8: Saintonge polychrome jug

Above: 9 Late medieval imported pottery.
1: Beauvais green-glazed dish; 2: Italian maiolica dish; 3: Italian maiolica jug; 4: Beauvais double-slipped sgrafitto jug; 5: Raeren stoneware mug; 6: Low Countries redware tripod cooking pot; 7: Saintonge chafing dish; 8: Tudor Green ware mug; 9: Valencian lustreware dish

Right: 10 Feast of the Duke de Berry. This New Year feast from the early fifteenth-century *Les Très Riches Heures du Duc de Berry* depicts the Duke with numerous guests and servants. Behind the table hangs a tapestry depicting a tournament. On the left a servant assists one guest to wash his hands

11 A fourteenth-century dining scene. This famous scene from the early fourteenth-century Luttrell Psalter depicts Sir Geoffrey Luttrell, his wife, daughter-in-law, two of his sons and two Dominican friars

12 Detail taken from 'The life and death of Sir Henry Unton'

13 Maiolica portrait dish, workshop
of Cornelis Lubberts, Haarlem 1483

14 Painting of meal given by grand vizier in the Topkapi Palace in honour of ambassador Cornelis Calkoen by
Jean-Baptiste Vanmour. *Amsterdam, Rijksmuseum A-4077*

15 Ottoman
miniature by
Levnî, *Surnâme-I
Vehbi*, Topkapi
Palace Museum
Library (fol 50a),
1712 AD

16 Humphry Repton's view of Longleat from Prospect Hill. *British Library 59.e.20 Longleat*

8 Grave relief of a family of men and women dining, Mainz, *c.*220–230

large round serving dishes of the size depicted on the reliefs was not a vessel type produced by the makers of samian ware.

FOOD AS A DISPLAY OF OPULENCE

There is much attention paid to the details of the food on the platters, so not only the vessels are a display of status, also the food is an indicator of wealth and luxury. The platters are ideal to present this culinary opulence. The reliefs show the moment when the food was brought into the dining room and placed on the table, perhaps for primary inspection and certainly to whet the appetite of the diners. This is also the moment described with great anticipation and wonder in descriptions of dining scenes by Horace (*Satires* 2.8) and Petronius (*Satyricon* 35–36, 40, 49, 69). An indication that the display of food was important in conveying the affluence and liberality of the host and promising pleasure to the guest is provided in the early third-century floor mosaics in the dining room at the House of the Buffet Supper in Antioch in Syria (*colour plate 2*). Here large oval and rectangular silver platters with food, from the first course of eggs, artichokes and pig trotters, through other courses of fish, ham, roast fowl and fruit, are depicted in the semi-circular apse just in front of and along the edge of the place

33

9 Marble sarcophagus of Publius Caecilius Vallianus in Rome showing servants bringing in food on large platters, third century AD

where the semi-circular dining couch, or stibadium, would have stood. Also on a third-century marble sarcophagus in Rome, wealth and abundance is depicted by servants carrying large platters containing a whole roast fowl and a roast lamb or piglet (*9*). Like the dining scene on the Igel monument, a whole cooked fish on a platter rests on the table. Neither the funerary reliefs, nor the other scenes, show the actual consumption of the meal, as this would have involved the whole chickens or fish being cut into small portions by the servants. Food cut up into bite-size morsels would have made for far less ostentatious display.

RELATIVE VALUES OF SERVING, DRINKING AND DINING VESSELS OF DIFFERING MATERIALS

In general, it is likely that the drinking, serving and dining paraphernalia represented on the funerary reliefs, both the *Totenmahl* scenes of the first century and the family dining scenes of the later second and third centuries, is meant to represent costly possessions. The literary sources are helpful in assessing which materials were considered precious, and which less valuable, in antiquity. According to Suetonius (*Claudius* 32), the emperor Claudius, for example, had a golden cup stolen from his table; the emperor invited the thief back the next day and ordered his servants to single this man out by serving him with an earthenware cup. Tacitus (*Histories* 1.48) recounts the same story, but adds to it by saying that the whole service given to the thief was of earthenware. Clearly, pottery dishes were chosen in this context to humiliate the guest. Although the banquet of the wealthy freedman Trimalchio is ficticious, Petronius provides us with information on the costly tablewares in the mid-first century AD. In his portrayal of the banquet, an entrée dish of silver, a silver chafing dish, silver cups and jugs, a silver grill and a silver ointment basin are brought into the dining room (*Satyricon* 31, 34, 35, 52, 70). 'Discoloured old silver', presumably the family silver, is mentioned in the fifth century by Sidonius Apollinaris in the context of costly dining (*Letters* 1.2). Other costly vessels were those made of crystal or of fluorspar (Petronius, *Satyricon* 64; Historia Augusta, *Lucius Verus* 5.2-5).

So what was considered less valuable? Roman assessments of glass are varied. According to Pliny (*Natural History* 36.198-99), glass had replaced gold and silver for drinking vessels, and he says that the most highly prized glass was transparent because it looked like the much more costly rock crystal. Perhaps what he means is that glass had become a very common material for drinking vessels, since silver was clearly still used. Seventy years before in the early first century AD, Strabo (*Geography* 16.2.25) wrote about glass that 'at Rome, a bowl or drinking cup may be purchased for a copper coin'. Presumably he was talking about simple, undecorated glass. Petronius (*Satyricon* 51) has Trimalchio say that he preferred glass: 'Glass at least does not smell like bronze. If it were not so breakable, I should prefer it to gold. As it is, it is so cheap.'

As far as ceramics are concerned, Juvenal (*Satires* 3) complained of the wealthy inhabitants of Rome being 'ashamed to eat off earthenware', although he also said that they would not find it 'unseemly if suddenly transported to the Marsi and a Sabine table', i.e. to a simple, country estate in mountainous central Italy. Pliny (*Natural History* 35.159-160) stressed the usefulness of clay for making a variety of items, such as wine jars, water pipes and roof tiles, and he claimed that 'Samian pottery is still esteemed for its tableware'. This glossy red tableware is praised almost certainly for its usefulness and quality, rather than its regard as a prestigious item. Martial (*Epigrams* 14.98; 14.108) wrote disparagingly of it, saying that servants need not be afraid to break it, but he advised people not to be too scornful of Arretine ware (from northern Italy). The 'stoic simplicity' of Quintus Tubero was marked by his use of 'shabby goat skins' and samian plates (*vasa Samia*) rather than fine cloth and silver dishes at a funeral feast in honour of Publius Africanus. This, according to Cicero (For *Murena* 75), was considered particularly mean and 'more appropriate for the death of Diogenes the Cynic than a banquet to honour the death of the mighty Africanus'. Pottery was clearly not considered a high-status tableware by wealthy Roman diners.

Some types of continental pottery, however, are often categorised by British archaeologists as high-status wares, particularly the glossy red samian ware. While samian ware has been shown by Steve Willis to have had some special status in Britain, it is not necessarily the case on the continent where the production centres were located. The very high output of this tableware suggests rather that it was a mass-produced item. It must be said that there is no indication whatever that any tablewares of this material are represented on any of the funerary monuments. The size of most of the tables, particularly the small round tripod tables, is hardly suitable to the use and display of sets of small plates, bowls and saucers so typical of samian, unless, of course, there were several tables allotted to a party of diners. Nor do the shapes of the vessels seen on the reliefs generally correspond to those of this type of ceramics.

But perhaps in considering whether the vessels depicted on the funerary reliefs might have been made of glass or pottery in imitation of metal prototypes we are missing the point. Anyone in antiquity who saw the scenes on these monuments would have known that precious metal vessels were the most prestigious, and they would have known that this is exactly what is alluded to. Whether or not the auxiliary and legionary soldiers could have afforded a silver drinking service, if they were not high-ranking officers (and none of the men commemorated by the gravestones discussed here was an officer), is possibly not so important. At least in choosing a commemorative image of themselves making use of such vessels they could be seen to have lived the good life of the socially prominent. The same applies to the civilian stones of the later second and third centuries. The large platters full of food used in the merchant-class households of the tomb owners may, in reality, have been made of cheaper glass, rather than silver, but the audiences of these scenes would have known that silver plate was the most desirable and expensive, and they would have 'translated' the images of such vessels into the precious metal services of the aristocrats.

CONCLUSION

This examination of funerary monuments depicting drinking and dining from the later first to the mid-third centuries AD in Gaul and Germany allows several conclusions to be drawn. Firstly, there is a noticeable change from the early heroic drinking scenes of soldiers adapted from eastern Mediterranean prototypes to high-status formal dining images developed for the tombs of wealthy civilians. Secondly, the strict gender division between male drinking and mixed-sex dining is bridged by the mid- to late second century. Although the convention of reclining or sitting at the table appears to be related to gender or social position, there may have been a relaxation of or a departure from the traditional customs maintained in the centre of the empire. Thirdly, the vessels used in drinking, eating and serving reflect contemporary material culture, but the range of vessels depicted is carefully selected to enhance the status and prestige of the participants. In all likelihood, the vessels depicted in the funerary scenes are those made of precious metals such as silver. Objects in these materials were a signal of great wealth and prestige. Finally, the presentation of food, and the inclusion of servants and slaves preparing and serving that food, is designed to display the affluence and liberality of the host within the context of competitive social activity. The 'theatre' for this activity was the dining room.

Maureen Carroll

ACKNOWLEDGEMENTS

Figures *1* and *4* are from the Rheinisches Bildarchiv; fig. *5* is after E. Zahn, *Die Igeler Säule bei Trier* (Neuss, 1976); fig. *6* is from the Rheinisches Landesmuseum, Bonn; fig. *7* is from the Museo Archeologico Nazionale, Naples; fig. *8* is from the Rheinisches Landesmuseum, Mainz; *colour plate 1* is from the Corning Museum of Glass; *colour plate 2* is from the Department of Art and Archaeology, Princeton University; fig. *9* is from the German Archaeological Institute, Rome; all other illustrations are by the author.

BIBLIOGRAPHY

Balzer, M., 'Die Alltagsdarstellungen der treverischen Grabdenkmäler', *Trierer Zeitschrift*, 46 (1983), pp.7-151

Carroll, M., *Romans, Celts and Germans. The German Provinces of Rome* (Stroud, 2001)

Drinkwater, J.F., 'The rise and fall of the Gallic Iulii: aspects of the development of the aristocracy of the Three Gauls under the early Empire', *Latomus*, 37 (1978), pp.817-850

— , 'The wool textile industry of Gallia Belgica and the Secundinii of Igel: questions and hypotheses', *Textile History*, 13/1 (1982), pp.111-128

Dunbabin, K.M.D., *The Roman Banquet. Images of Conviviality* (Cambridge, 2003)

Ellis, S., 'Late-antique dining: architecture, furnishings and behaviour', in R. Laurence and A. Wallace-Hadrill (eds), *Domestic Space in the Roman World: Pompeii and Beyond* (Portsmouth, 1997), pp.41-51

Klatt, U., 'Römische Klapptische. Drei- und vierbeinige Stützgestelle aus Bronze und Silber', *Kölner Jahrbuch*, 28 (1995), 349-574

Knudsen, S. 'Dining as a fine art: tablewares of the Ancient Romans', in C. Kondoleon (ed.), *Antioch. The Lost Ancient city* (Princeton, 2000), pp.181–195

Mols, S.T.A.M., 'Identification of the woods used in the furniture at Herculaneum', in W.F. Jashemski and F.G. Meyer (eds), *The Natural History of Pompeii* (Cambridge, 2002), pp.225–234

Noelke, P., 'Zur Chronologie der Grabreliefs mit Mahldarstellung im römischen Germanien', in H. Walter (ed.), *La sculpture d'époque romaine dans le Nord, dans l'Est des Gaules et dans les régions avoisinantes* (Paris, 2000), pp.59–70

Strong, D., *Greek and Roman Gold and Silver Plate* (London, 1966)

Van Lith, M.E., 'First-century Cantharoi with a stemmed foot: Their distribution and social context', in M. Newby and K. Painter (eds), *Roman Glass: Two Centuries of Art and Invention* (London, 1991), pp.99–110

Willis, S., 'Samian: beyond dating', in K. Meadows et al. (eds), *Proceedings of the Sixth Annual Theoretical Roman Archaeology Conference*, 1996 (Oxford, 1997), pp.38–54

three

COOKING LIKE A NATIVE, DINING LIKE A ROMAN: FOOD PREPARATION AND CONSUMPTION IN ROMAN SWITZERLAND

In the regions north of the Alps, the Roman period is regarded as a time when the peoples of the Late Iron Age experienced considerable cultural change, adapting their own culture in many ways to that of the Mediterranean. This assumption also pertains to cultural customs surrounding the preparation and consumption of food and drink. Such customs can be reconstructed by an assessment of the remains of vessels, primarily made of pottery, which are the most frequently encountered artefacts surviving in all excavations. Using the example of the pottery from Baden (*Aquae Helveticae*), a small Roman town (or *vicus*) in Switzerland, this chapter will examine whether Mediterranean eating and drinking habits actually were fully adopted in the wake of Roman conquest.

The *vicus* of *Aquae Helveticae* lies in central Switzerland, in the territory of the Helvetii (*civitas Helvetiorum*), about 4 miles east of the Roman legionary camp of Vindonissa (*10*). As the Latin name suggests, a natural thermal water source existed here that was tapped in the Roman period, and possibly even earlier. The Roman town above this source was established at the beginning of the first century AD, with occupation continuing until the late third century. In the late Roman period, the baths of the thermal spa were enclosed within a wall, however the earlier settlement area to the west appears to have been abandoned by this time. Continuous occupation at the site of the thermal source is likely, whereas the medieval town of Baden sprang up further south in a different location.

Tacitus (*Histories* I.67) records that the place was sacked and destroyed in AD 69 by the twenty-first legion stationed in Vindonissa. A thick layer of burnt material, attesting to this destruction, has been found in archaeological excavations.

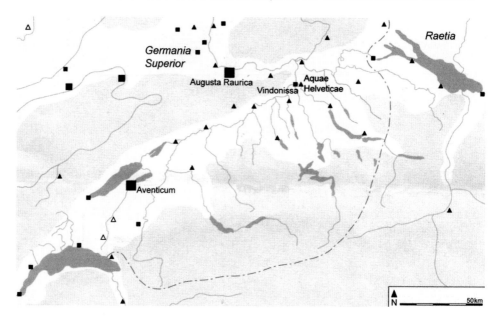

10 Map showing the location of *Aquae Helveticae*/Baden in Switzerland

During fieldwork in 1977, excavators revealed densely stratified deposits, and they were able to recognise 15 phases of occupation spanning some 200 years, from the period between AD 5-10 and AD 205-210. These excavations provided twelve assemblages of diagnostic finds with which pottery development can be followed from one generation to the next, from the early first to the late second century AD.

CERAMICS: THE NEW AND THE TRADITIONAL

To be able to recognise the different traditions, both native and Mediterranean, in dining and drinking the Gallo-Roman pottery from Baden must be compared not only with the pottery of the Late Iron Age but also with the ceramics in use in the first century BC in Italy. Usefully, in addition to the wide range of artefacts surviving in the archaeological record, the array of vessels used in the Mediterranean at that time is referred to in ancient literary sources. Mediterranean tablewares included plates and platters, bowls and small sauce dishes, while drinking vessels took the form of cups, beakers and flagons. In preparing food, cooking pots, cooking bowls, baking platters, as well as grinding bowls for mixing spices (*mortaria*) were used (*11*). Storage vessels included amphorae, globular jars (*dolia*), jars, and large jugs with more than one handle.

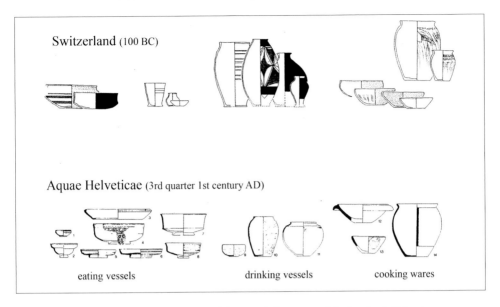

Switzerland (100 BC)

Aquae Helveticae (3rd quarter 1st century AD)

eating vessels   drinking vessels   cooking wares

11 Pottery forms of the late La Tène period (*c.*100 BC) from central Switzerland (*Schweizer Mittelland*), and of the third quarter of the first century AD from *Aquae Helveticae*/Baden. Scale around 1:10

The vessel repertoire in Celtic regions and in the northwest provinces is known primarily through the context of graves, where these vessels were deposited with the dead (*13, 14*). In the pre-Roman period, pottery forms used in eating included dishes with incurved rims and bowls, while those used for drinking comprised pear-shaped jars, bottles and carinated beakers. Vessels used to prepare and store food were cooking pots, cooking dishes with incurved rims, and jars. In addition to serving vessels such as bowls, bottles and pear-shaped jars, there are other forms of small vessels that suggest that people north of the Alps used individual sets of vessels. This is probably true also of the Roman period, when dishes, especially dining plates, are found that were labelled with an inscribed name or mark of the owner.

If we compare the pottery forms as they appeared in central Switzerland (*Schweizer Mittelland*) around 100 BC to an assemblage of the third quarter of the first century AD from Aquae Helveticae (*11*), it can be seen that the eating vessels of the later period are now largely made up of new forms, namely Roman types. These include flat, small and large platters, small sauce dishes and bowls. The old forms, however, do not disappear. Carinated bowls and dishes with incurved rims are still used, and although new forms of drinking vessels do appear, such as cups and flagons, typical Iron Age forms like bottles, pear-shaped jars and carinated beakers continue to be found. Vessels for use in the kitchen, especially cooking pots, largely comprise well-known types that had a longer tradition in

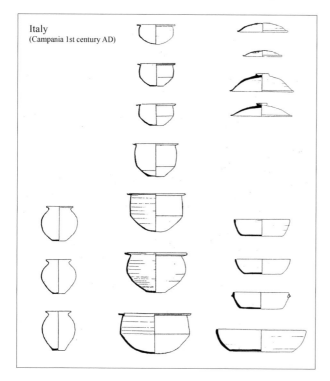

Italy
(Campania 1st century AD)

12 Cooking wares from Italy.
Scale around 1:5

the region: cooking jars and dishes with incurved rims. The only new forms to be found are mortaria, in which sauces were mixed, so-called honey-jars (small storage jars with two handles), and *dolia* (large globular storage vessels). However, it is clear that in Italy people cooked their food in very different types of vessel, such as large, wide bowls and large flat platters with fitted lids (*12*), and these types do not appear in Aquae Helveticae.

It is apparent, therefore, that there was not complete acculturation of eating and drinking customs. Before the last third of the first century AD, around 40 per cent of the vessels were still rooted in the native tradition. Towards the end of that century we can see a slight decrease to around 30 per cent, but this level was more or less constant right up until the late second century AD. The Romanization of food-related customs occurred at different rates and to differing degrees depending on the type of vessel (*colour plate 2*). For example, pottery vessels used for eating were largely made up of new forms, already 70 per cent in the early and middle first century AD, and as much as 80 per cent in the second century. In contrast, the drinking vessels present a very different picture. The new forms used in drinking comprise only 30-40 per cent in the first century, and moreover there seems to be a resurgence of the native forms in the second century. In the first century between 60-80 per cent of cooking

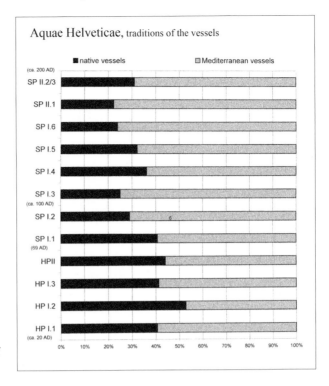

13 *Aquae Helveticae.* Traditions of vessel types I

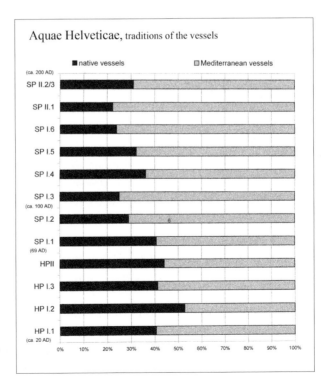

14 *Aquae Helveticae.* Traditions of vessel types II

vessels are of native type, but the prevalence decreases to 30 per cent in the second century.

A LIMITED ADOPTION OF NEW WAYS OF CONSUMING

An examination of the repertoire of new vessel types is warranted, before the composition of the actual types of vessel are analysed in detail. All the forms in use in the Mediterranean during the late first century BC were adopted at Baden with the exception of one type: the large bowl with two handles (15). One of the only places it is found in the *Schweizer Mittelland* is in the legionary camp of Vindonissa, where it has been interpreted not as a vessel for food preparation or consumption but as a wash basin. The range of the new forms of eating vessels is similar to that of Italy, especially the small and large platters and the sauce dishes (16). The only significant difference in the vessel repertoires in Baden is the bowl. In the first half of the first century AD, bowls appear about as frequently as in Italy, but from the last third of that century they occur in twice the quantity as in Italy. It is, perhaps, not surprising since the main form of the native repertoire in Baden is the bowl. This vessel type makes up around 15 per cent of the pottery forms there in the first century AD, dropping slightly to 5-10 per cent in the second century.

When the drinking vessels are examined (17), a very different picture from that of Italy emerges. The drinking-cup, the Mediterranean beaker and the flagon do not totally replace the native forms of vessels used in drinking and serving, namely the beaker, bottle and pear-shaped jar. When the cooking vessels are considered (18), it appears that they are more frequent in the Mediterranean than in Baden, especially in the second century AD. However, the mortarium, one of the main indications of Romanization in food preparation, occurs no more frequently in Italy than it does in Baden. Wide bowls and large cooking platters, that supplant the high cooking jars during the first century in the southern part of the Roman Empire, had only a moderate impact in Switzerland. Meanwhile, the Italian custom of closing vessels with a lid also occurs at Baden in the second century AD.

CONCLUSION

What does this review of vessel forms reveal about the acculturation of cooking, dining and drinking customs? First, it can be deduced that the custom of refining food with sauces, as in the Mediterranean, was received well in Roman

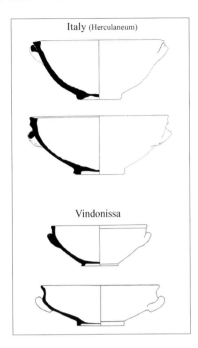

15 Wash basins from Italy
and Vindonissa. Scale 1:4

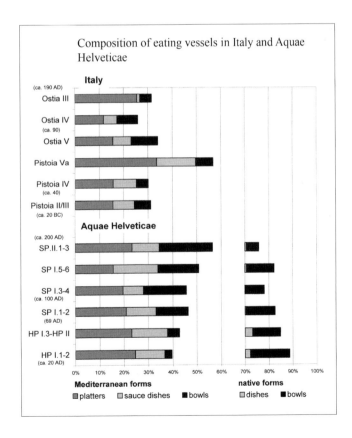

16 Composition of eating
vessels in Italy and in *Aquae
Helveticae*/Baden

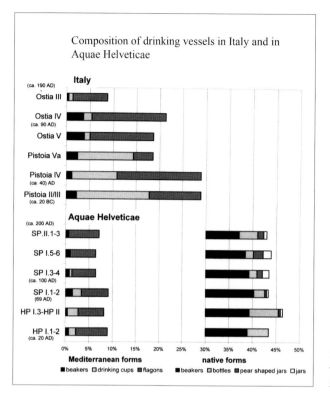

17 Composition of drinking vessels in Italy and in *Aquae Helveticae*/Baden

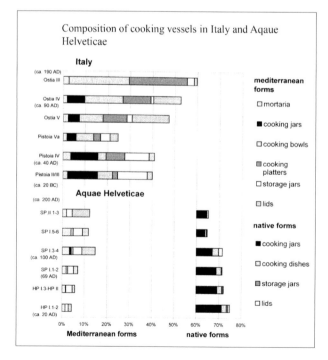

18 Composition of cooking vessels in Italy and in *Aquae Helveticae*/Baden

Switzerland. Second, and in contrast, food was apparently seldom cooked in flat, wide vessels, as was increasingly the case in Italy. Instead cooking took place in the well-known high, narrow cooking jars. This may be due to very traditional methods of cooking food, in a broth with a lot of liquid. It must be assumed that the meals cooked in these vessels were soups and broth made from cereals and pulses, especially millet, barley and horse beans, to which a little meat and kale was added. This would explain the continuing need for deep bowls used in serving food, and also why they could not be replaced by the flat, wide platter, the Mediterranean serving vessel par excellence. If individual dining vessels and serving vessels are differentiated, in other words small platters and large platters, it can be seen that the larger examples slowly disappear. A reason for the adherence to the traditional way of cooking might be that food went cold faster when served 'dry' on flat plates than it did in deep bowls, especially when the food was not kept in a hot broth.

Although the consumption of wine increased in Roman times, this is not clearly reflected in the repertoire of drinking vessels such as flagons and, in the first century AD, by the use of open drinking cups. The popularity of beakers, especially those with a high body and a narrow mouth, or, in the second century AD, those with a high neck, demonstrates that native drinks, such as beer, did not lose their importance.

It can be said, in conclusion, that during the Roman period in Switzerland an attempt was made to lay the table in the Italian style, with forms inspired from the Mediterranean. These included small and large platters and flagons. The custom of refining foods with sauces was also adopted. From now on mortaria and sauce dishes were part of the repertoire of vessels used. Wine was appreciated, but it did not prevail totally over the traditional beverages such as beer. However, the native tradition of cooking, in a broth, and ultimately eating and drinking, was strongly adhered to, perhaps because, in this climate, one preferred to eat the food while it was still hot. It might even be said that the Romanization of Switzerland has only happened recently, thanks to the huge success of Mediterranean cuisine in our own time. Olive oil and pizza spring to mind!

Caty Schucany

ACKNOWLEDGEMENTS

I would like to thank Andrew Lawrence for translating this paper into English. *Colour plate 3* is from P. Herman, *Bodenfunde aus Basels Ur- und Frühgeschichte* (Basel, 1983), p.31; fig. *11* is after F. Müller, G. Lüscher and G. Kaenel, *Die Schweiz vom*

Paläolithikum bis zum frühen Mittelalter SPM IV, Eisenzeit (Basel, 1999) fig. *83*, and after *Chronologie,* Antiqua 15 (Basel, 1986) p.236; *colour plate 4* is from M. Hartmann und H. Weber, *Die Römer im Aargau* (Aarau/Frankfurt a.M./Salzburg, 1985), fig. *59*; fig. *12* is after V. Di Giovanni, 'Produzione e consumo di ceramica da cucina nella Campania romana (II a.C.- II d.C.)', in M. Bats, *Les céramiques communes de Campanie et de Narbonnaise (Ier s. Av. J.-C. – IIe s. Apr. J.-C.). La vaiselle de cuisine et de table.* Collection du centre Jean Bérard, 14 (Naples, 1996), pp.65-103, fig. *9, 13, 18, 25*; fig. *15* is after L.A. Scatozza Höricht, 'Appunti sulla ceramica commune di Ercolano. Vasselame da cucina e recipienti per la preparazione degli alimenti', in M. Bats, *Les céramiques communes de Campanie et de Narbonnaise (Ier s. Av. J.-C. – IIe s. Apr. J.-C.). La vaiselle de cuisine et de table.* Collection du centre Jean Bérard, 14 (Naples, 1996), pp.129-156, fig. *9*, and E. Ettlinger and C. Simonett, *Römische Keramik aus dem Schutthügel von Vindonissa.* Veröffentlichungen der Gesellschaft Pro Vindonissa, 3 (Basel, 1952), Pl. 7. All other figures are by the author.

BIBLIOGRAPHY

Hilgers, W., *Lateinische Gefäßnamen. Bezeichnungen, Funktion und Form römischer Gefäße nach den antiken Schriftquellen* (Düsseldorf, 1969)

Schucany, C., 'Tradition indigène – tradition méditerranéenne: un essai appliqué à la céramique des Ier et IIe siècles d'Aquae Helveticae (Baden, Suisse)', *Société Française d'Étude de la Céramique Antique en Gaule. Actes du congrès de Versailles 20-23 mai 1993* (Marseille, 1993), pp.249-266

— , 'Eine Grabanlage im römischen Gutshof von Biberist-Spitalhof', *Archäologie der Schweiz*, 18 (1995), pp.142-154

— , *Aquae Helveticae. Zum Romanisierungsprozess am Beispiel des römischen Baden* (Grabung 1977) (Basel, 1996)

— , 'An elite funerary enclosure in the centre of the villa of Biberist-Spitalhof (Switzerland) – a case study', in M. Millett, J. Pearce and M. Struck (eds), *Burial, Society and context in the Roman World* (Oxford, 2000), pp.118-124

four

DINING *AL FRESCO* WITH THE LIVING AND THE DEAD IN ROMAN ITALY

People used to eat in winter by the hearth, in summer out-of-doors.
(Varro, *Life of the Roman People*, I)

In the ancient Roman world, dining occurred in a variety of contexts. Meals were often essentially private affairs, taking place in a domestic setting but also in public, such as during the often lavish banquets thrown by influential members of society to celebrate triumphs, anniversaries or their beneficence to their fellow citizens. On a less elaborate scale, semi-public dining took place in the many inns and wine shops of Italian towns and cities. Boundaries were often blurred, with private dinners between friends potentially taking place in public environments, such as a tavern, and semi-public activities involving invited guests occurring within the private house of the host. Religious ceremonies frequently involved ritual feasting, and meals were consumed as part of the rites accorded to the dead.

It is relatively unsurprising that *al fresco* dining was common in Roman Italy, particularly in the Bay of Naples where the climate was as conducive to eating outside then as it is today. In her comprehensive study of the ancient gardens of Pompeii and Herculaneum, Wilhelmina Jashemski repeatedly observes parallels between ancient and modern Pompeian lifestyle, including an enduring desire to conduct daily activities, particularly eating, in the open air. Pompeii furnishes us with much evidence for ancient *al fresco* dining, especially within a domestic context. Public banquets were held in areas capable of accommodating vast numbers of people, such as the Forum, but they leave little trace of their existence, not least because the structures involved were intended to be of a temporary nature. It is the very durability of domestic *al fresco* dining facilities that signals the importance attached to such activity and the desire to eat outside on a regular basis. Similar structures are also found in association with tombs and funerary monuments and attest to regular dining within the cemetery. In the majority of instances this is an activity that, by virtue of the required grave-side location, took place in the open air. An examination of such dining in both a domestic and funerary context allows us to better understand these occasions and their social nuances. It also elucidates the fact that at times domestic *al fresco* dining had more in common with funerary feasts than traditional indoor events or lavish public banquets.

RECLINING TO DINE IN ROMAN ITALY

During the early years of the Republic seated dining remained customary but by the first century BC it had become common practice to recline. The original Greek practice of reclining on couches appears to have been initially adopted by the aristocracy, but soon came to be widely considered as the only respectable way to dine. Indeed, according to Katherine Dunbabin, reclining was itself a symbol of prestige and privilege. The dining rooms (*triclinia*) in which banqueting activities were held were arranged with three broad couches placed at right angles to one another to form a rectilinear U-shape (also known as a *triclinium*). Occasionally the *triclinium* took the form of a permanent structure but was more commonly composed of three movable couches. Three diners lay diagonally across each couch (nine was considered the ideal number for a dinner party) in accordance with a strict order of precedence. The traditional place of honour was on the left side of the middle, or joining, couch adjacent to the host who reclined at the top of the lowest couch.

Yvon Thébert describes this arrangement as 'coded space' and in this capacity it not only lent to the proceedings a heightened degree of formality but affirmed the hierarchy of persons present and consequently contributed to the social negotiations that occurred during the meal. These social negotiations were what made dining so important in the eyes of Roman society. Banquets were often less about eating than they were self-advertisement and social promotion. For the host of a banquet such an occasion offered an opportunity to display visually their wealth, status and taste through the decor of the dining room, the food provided, the tableware upon which it was served, the social standing of the guests and various types of entertainment, ranging from poetry or philosophy readings to musicians and dancers. Furthermore, it was the right of the host to express their personal opinions on a variety of subjects and to enlighten guests with their own outlook on life and personal philosophies. Trimalchio, the *nouveau riche* former slave of Petronius' *Satyricon*, provides a glimpse in the first century AD of the rather extreme lengths to which it was possible for the host to go in order to try and impress upon his guests his wealth and knowledge. Although Trimalchio betrays his lowly origins many times in his attempt to *appear* cultured and educated, it is the way in which the trappings and protocol of the dinner party facilitate his desire to appear knowledgeable and superior that is significant. It is unlikely that the exaggerated actions of Trimalchio accurately reflect reality, but they do illustrate the significance of the dinner party as a tool for prescribed social interaction and negotiation. This was not restricted to the host, for guests were equally encouraged to express their views, although politeness and concerns about furthering their own position may have conspired to limit the extent to which they actively competed with their host. Consequently, banquets provided highly structured opportunities for networking on a variety of social, political, and probably financial, levels. Undoubtedly there were many occasions during which groups of friends simply enjoyed one another's company and good entertainment, or families came together to eat and perhaps celebrate religious festivals. However, even during these more intimate occasions, the strict conventions and customs of dining served as an arena in which social and familial hierarchies and relationships were established and renewed.

The ways in which dining activities communicated aspects of identity and status and contributed towards the establishment of social hierarchies is further illuminated by those that occurred in a truly public setting, during which the audience was considerably widened, often to include the entire population of a town or city. Public banquets thrown by wealthy members of the elite demonstrated to the populace their affluence and confirmed their position as important members of that society. However, the existence of such events also further emphasises the important concept of 'being seen to dine', or, more accurately, to recline. These occasions became public spectacles, reinforcing the social hierarchy by visibly distinguishing between different groups. Not everyone reclined at such occasions, for example, and those of lower status received a markedly different quantity and quality of food.

Dining activities were evidently deeply embedded within the Roman system of social relations. However, what happened when such activities moved out of the hierarchical confines of the dining room and into the open air?

EATING IN THE GARDEN

Although public banquets took place out-of-doors, they occurred far less frequently than those within the relative privacy of the household garden. The clearest evidence for *al fresco* dining at home is provided by the many dining structures built in the gardens of Pompeii in Campania, although sites elsewhere in Italy, and depictions in literary sources and art, attest to its prevalence outside Campania. Most commonly these facilities take the form of a masonry *triclinium* (three couches) or *biclinium* (two couches). The design of these structures duplicates those of indoor *triclinia*, with three couches of equal length flanking a small table. Often a small ledge runs around the interior for drinking cups and glasses. One of the best-preserved examples is that of the House of the Ephebe, which is set against a painted backdrop with a nymphaeum and fountain that allowed water to run between the diners. The *triclinium* itself is lavishly decorated with painted Egyptian scenes, indicating that many others may also have originally been decorated.

Fountains and pools feature highly in outdoor *triclinia*. The so-called House of the Silver Wedding (the home of Albucius Celsus) contained three indoor dining rooms in addition to an outdoor *triclinium* situated beside a large rectangular pool with a fountain at its centre. The circular white marble table also doubled as a fountain. This pleasant arrangement appears to have been appreciated by at least one guest (albeit a rather destructive one) who has scratched 'How inviting is your house, O Albucius' on the garden wall. Water also features in the garden of the House of Loreius Tiburtinus where the *biclinium* is located at the end of a long stretch of water, broken up by small bridges, an elaborate fountain, several small pools and flanked by small marble statues. Plates may have been floated on the pool which lay between the couches (*colour plate 5*). In the garden of the House of Julia Felix diners reclined on marble faced couches in front of a stepped fountain, with the water reappearing in the centre of the triclinium. Not all outdoor dining facilities at Pompeii include elaborate water features, but it is evident that wherever possible water was integrated within their design. This not only contributed towards the creation of a pleasant environment, but also displayed the host's ability to squander precious water on mere luxury. The completion of an aqueduct in the early first century AD greatly increased Pompeian access to water and may have lessened the impact of such frivolous display. Garden *triclinia* with water features are known from elsewhere in Italy, for example at Hadrian's villa near Tivoli and the elaborate *triclinium* located in the centre of a large fishpond at the mouth of the grotto at Sperlonga where the Emperor Tiberius narrowly escaped a fatal rockfall. Examples have been identified at Ostia (*19*), and Pliny the Younger's description (in his *Letters*, 5.6)

19 Garden *biclinium* and pool, Ostia

of his Tuscan villa includes details of an open-air *triclinium* adjacent to a pool on which food was floated. Indoor *triclinia* occasionally feature small fountains or cascades. Even the briefest description of such settings conjures up pleasant images of dining in luxurious surroundings, considerably less formal than the sumptuously decorated yet austere indoor triclinium.

The majority of outdoor facilities were shaded by vine-covered pergolas. These structures rarely survive, but post holes and root cavities attest their prevalence. The above examples were all shaded by a pergola, as were many of the less elaborate examples found in Pompeii (*20*, *21*). When the time of day that dining took place is examined the functional characteristics of these pergolas become clearer. Both breakfast (*ientaculum*) and lunch (*prandium*) were light meals eaten at various times and with little ceremony. The *cena* (main meal) was usually eaten around 3 or 4 o'clock in the afternoon, depending on the season and the status of the diners. For those eating outside, the pergola provided shade from the afternoon sun in addition to heightening the sense of being 'close to nature'. Dinner parties doubtless continued long into the evening, and provision for lighting has been identified in several Pompeian gardens. Movable lighting was probably also brought from inside when required.

Permanent provisions were not necessarily required in order to eat out-of-doors. Movable couches were used for indoor *triclinia*, and there is little reason

20 Reconstructed pergola shading diners reclining on a *triclinium*, House of Hercules, Pompeii

21 Vine-covered pergola shading the *triclinium* of the House of Sallust, Pompeii

to assume that on occasion such furniture was not transferred to the garden. The imprints of wooden *triclinia* were recovered from the peristyle garden of the House of Menander in Pompeii and that of another house in the next block. Although these may have been permanent garden features they illustrate the fact that less substantial furniture was used for outdoor dining and could be located in various positions. Even more temporary furnishings, in the form of bolsters and cushions placed directly on the ground, may also have been used. Scenes depicting outdoor dining in this way indicate that even soft furnishings tended to be arranged in the traditional U-shape and, therefore, that concepts of proper reclining and orders of precedence may have been retained within less formal settings. The flexibility offered by less permanent arrangements implies that outdoor dining was not necessarily restricted to wealthier members of society with elaborate gardens at their disposal.

Before the issue of *who* dined outside can be examined further, it is important to note the existence at Pompeii of one semicircular masonry couch (a *stibadium*) in the garden of the House of Adonis. Katherine Dunbabin has argued that this form of couch originated specifically for use in an outdoor context before eventually being adopted for indoor use during later centuries. Drawing on images depicting scenes of outdoor banquets where diners are shown reclining on cushions or semicircular bolsters placed on the ground, she suggests that this was the customary arrangement for outdoor dining, the cushions often being replaced by permanent semicircular structures. Such occasions were, she explains, more relaxed than those which took place within the formal atmosphere of the indoor *triclinium*, replete with its rectilinear couches, order of precedence and enclosing walls. However, the existence of only a single example of a permanent *stibadium* at Pompeii during the period in which it was supposedly the preferred option for outdoor dining perhaps suggests that it was less of an established arrangement than Dunbabin asserts. Although artistic depictions of outdoor meals suggest that semicircular arrangements were common, it must be remembered that not only did limited understandings of perspective (clearly illustrated by many examples of Roman art) prevent an accurate re-creation of the rectilinear *triclinium*, but the simple informality of dining on the ground naturally lent itself to a less regular shape. The right angles of the traditional *triclinium* are created only by the furniture itself; if the diners reclining upon it were transplanted on to the ground their arrangement would automatically appear to take on a less angular shape. Those depicted reclining on cushions would naturally appear to be doing so in a semicircular arrangement in contrast to the regular impression given by a *triclinium*. The prevalence of 'regular' garden *triclinia* (and *biclinia*) at Pompeii implies that it was not considered essential for outdoor diners to arrange themselves in a semicircular fashion. In fact, excavation revealed that the garden *biclinium* of the House of Loreius Tiburtinus had been preceded by a masonry triclinium, presumably removed during a re-landscaping of the garden, with no evidence of a *stibadium*. Had the owners wished to comply with strict traditions of semicircular outdoor dining, it seems curious that neither of these structures adopted such a form. However, the implication that dining in such a way created a more relaxed atmosphere remains important. Perhaps dining outside in any form was considered less rigid than indoors, given the pleasant natural environment in which it occurred and the flexibility it offered. The masonry *triclinia* and *biclinia* may therefore be an attempt to make such occasions more formal and in keeping with respectable dining practice.

The popularity of eating in the open air evidently spanned the entire social spectrum. Where indications of permanent structures are lacking it can be assumed that temporary facilities were used, and the existence of outdoor dining facilities in conjunction with the city's commercial establishments, including inns and vineyards, indicates that it was widely considered desirable to eat *al fresco*. Although Pompeian taverns retained areas in which customers could stand or sit in order to eat and drink, several also provided formal dining facilities in the form of both indoor and outdoor triclinia. A small inn situated just inside the Porta di Ercolano, for instance, was equipped with both an indoor and outdoor *triclinium*, the latter located beneath a vine-covered pergola. Many other examples can be found scattered throughout the city along with several of the large vineyards and were probably available for hire. The *triclinia* within the large vineyards near the amphitheatre were perhaps hired by visitors attending the games. They may also have been used by clubs or groups of friends for official banquets, celebrations and meetings. There was evidently a strong desire to eat *outside* as evidenced by the fact that many indoor triclinia have paintings of gardens adorning their walls. These paintings created the illusion of dining outside.

How was the act of dining affected by its relocation outside? Dunbabin points to the examples of Hortensius and Lucullus as instances of wealthy Romans from the late Republic developing the occasion of *al fresco* dining as an opportunity for elaborate display and sumptuous hospitality, banqueting as they did within wild beast parks and aviaries. Yet it should be noted that the success of the latter venture is questioned by Varro in his treatise *On Farming* when he comments that 'the birds flying inside the windows give less pleasure than the intrusive smell, filling the nostrils, gives annoyance'. Although such exuberance was probably restricted to the wealthiest members of society, it remains possible that standard outdoor dining operated in a similar, albeit substantially reduced, manner. The luxurious setting and design of many facilities at Pompeii has been illustrated, with complex water features and decorated *triclinia* occurring frequently in garden environments. These may have functioned in a similar way to those of the indoor *triclinium*, allowing the host to demonstrate their wealth, taste and culture through the display of art and luxurious paintings or features. The gardens themselves were equally intertwined in this process, both their design and layout, operating in conjunction with the often striking paintings found on their walls, capable of communicating the impeccable taste or sheer wealth of the host. In large urban areas, where space was at a premium, a garden represented considerable wealth and standing in society and entertaining guests *within* this environment would have further impressed upon them the status of the host.

However, the garden was also a place in which one could escape the prescribed confines of the house, something that was perhaps paralleled by dining practice. As Nicholas Purcell has observed, the garden 'offered a new dimension of flexibility: soft and changing natural elements or open spaces and vistas could be substituted for any of the fixed, artificial, hard constituents of the ordinary interior'. The indoor dining room, often considered the most important reception room of the house, was one such fixed place. This was the room in which the host exhibited who they were, and who they wanted to be. The garden, with its more relaxed and intimate environment, created a greater sense of informality, whilst its structure and layout still operated to maintain an atmosphere of luxury, wealth and culture.

This informality is supported considering *who* dined out-of-doors. Jashemski proposes that formal entertaining took place indoors, even during the summer months, unquestionably because this was the prime function of the indoor *triclinium*. Had this room been of reduced significance then one would expect this to be reflected by its décor, size and location, but at Pompeii it remains the main reception room, as evidenced by its opulent decoration. Consequently, it is unlikely that outdoor *triclinia* were used for formal banquets of considerable importance. If the host wished to truly demonstrate their culture, taste, wealth and social status to guests of particular importance they would have done so within the traditionally formal and hierarchical space set aside for such purposes within the house. Who, then, ate in the garden? The owner of the house and his family undoubtedly dined outside on a regular basis. Indeed, it has been suggested that one Pompeian *triclinium* with a lower extension on one of the couches was designed specifically to allow the children of the family to participate in *al fresco* meals. The veracity of this claim is somewhat uncertain, given the fact that a lowered section of the couch would have been a short-term requirement, until the child grew up, and would have seriously limited its use for adult gatherings. Presumably the family were joined on occasion by other extended family members and friends. It remains possible that clients were occasionally entertained out-of-doors, but it is unlikely that the garden regularly formed the backdrop for formal banquets of great significance. Their display was instead directed towards impressing friends and affirming to themselves, rather than the stranger, their own identity. As a result, the atmosphere of *al fresco* dining was far more relaxed than its indoor counterpart.

MEALS WITH THE DEAD

Outdoor dining was equally associated with the cemetery where meals were consumed in the company of the living and the dead. Dining was intimately involved in funerary ritual and commemoration. On the day of the funeral it was customary for the family to consume a meal (the *silicernium*) at the grave, an activity that was repeated nine days later (the *cena novemdialis*) in order to signal the end of the mourning period. These activities, which included the giving of food to the dead in the form of libations or liquid offerings, were considered essential for allowing them to pass comfortably into the world of the dead. Vengeful spirits who did not receive such rites posed a threat to the living, as a cautionary tale recounted by the Augustan poet Ovid reminds us (*Fasti*, II. 547-556). He also provides an insight into another occasion on which meals were consumed in the cemetery: the *Parentalia*. This festival required families to return to the grave with offerings for the dead. Ovid (*Fasti*, II. 533-542) describes the necessary action:

> Appease the souls of your fathers and bring small gifts to the tombs erected to them. Ghosts ask but little: they value piety more than a costly gift ... A tile wreathed with votive garlands, a sprinkling of corn, a few grains of salt, bread soaked in wine, and some loose violets, these are offerings enough: set these on a potsherd and leave it in the middle of the road. Not that I forbid larger offerings, but even these suffice to appease the shades: add prayers and the appropriate words at the hearths set up for the purpose.

Afterwards the family again reprised the funerary meal in the company of their dead relatives. Ritual meals were also eaten at the place of burial to commemorate the birthday and death of the deceased. Literary sources provide ample evidence for the observance of these activities, as do funerary inscriptions that often outline the duties of an heir. The will of a man from Andamentunum (modern Langres), for instance, asks that annual contributions be made by his family and freed slaves in order to pay for banquets at the tomb on the first day of April, May, June, July, August and October. The dead were certainly not neglected.

The extent to which wishes such as these were actually carried out by the survivors of the deceased can be called into question. However, archaeology provides a considerable amount of evidence for dining in the cemetery. Tombs

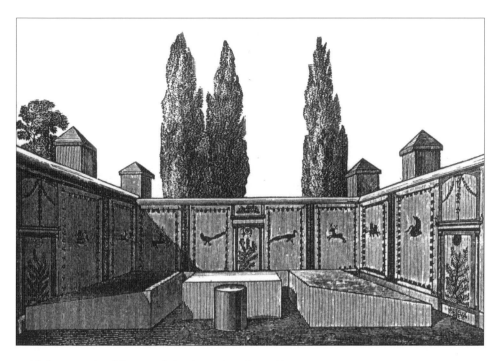

22 Triclinium tomb of Gnaeus Vibrius Saturninus, Pompeii

located in the cemeteries of Pompeii are known to include actual dining facilities. The best known, is that of Gnaeus Vibrius Saturninus on the Street of the Tombs, which has a masonry *triclinium* and table situated within an enclosure. The interior walls of the enclosure were painted with images of plants, animals and birds (*22*). The cemeteries of Ostia and Isola Sacra (located on the major road linking Rome's ports of Ostia and Portus) provide further confirmation of the importance of funerary dining. Several tombs in the Via Laurentina cemetery at Ostia contain *triclinia* within their enclosures (*23*). One of these (Tomb 31) also contained a wall painting depicting named banqueters with raised glasses evidently taking part in funerary dining activities. The cemetery of Isola Sacra offers an even greater amount of evidence for permanent dining structures. Here the couches take the form of *biclinia* and are located outside the tomb entrance, most commonly flanking the doorway, and often with a masonry block that may have been used either as a table or altar for funerary offerings (*24* and *colour plate 6*). Such structures are most often associated with the larger house tombs of the cemetery (built by freed slaves for themselves, their family and their own freed slaves) (*25*), although some of the smaller tombs belonging to less wealthy individuals also exhibit masonry couches or table supports. Evidently all levels of society were eager to provide structures specifically for use in funerary

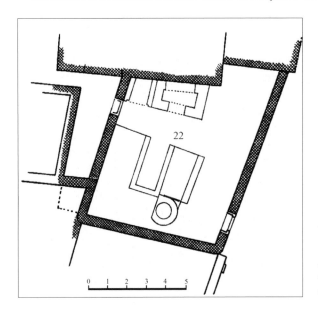

23 Plan of funerary *triclinium* and well in Tomb 22, Via Laurentina, Ostia

banqueting rituals. Furthermore, ovens and wells have been located at both Isola Sacra and Via Laurentina and indicate that food preparation regularly took place at these sites. It again remains possible that dining activities could take place without durable structures. Movable furniture was used in domestic *al fresco* dining contexts, and groups often reclined on the ground. There is therefore little reason to assume that a lack of permanent facilities indicates that banquets did not occur. Perhaps poorer members of the community should be imagined conducting feasts in the form of picnics.

It is again important to ask who was involved in these activities, how their location affected the atmosphere of such occasions and their role in social negotiation. There is little reason to believe that the very wealthy and very poor held radically different beliefs that prevented them from dining at the graveside. The physical manifestation of these activities may have differed, but all social groups within the community were eager to observe such rites regardless of their wealth, legal status or social standing. Tombs and funerary monuments could directly communicate aspects of the identity, status, wealth, culture and aspirations of the owner and their family to other members of the Roman community. Acting in a similar manner to the indoor *triclinium* of a domestic house, they allowed the owner to continue to advertise unequivocally who he was (or wanted to be). The tomb remained an active element in the life of the family, thus allowing the surviving members to also capitalise on the opportunities it provided for display and the perpetuation of memory. The fact that cemeteries were visited frequently by various people taking part in funerals

24 *Biclinium* outside Tomb 15, Isola Sacra

25 House tombs with *biclinia*, Isola Sacra

and observing post-funeral rites, in addition to their location adjacent to major roads, increased their communicative power. Seen in this context, dining in the cemetery becomes increasingly important. Although some funerary dining facilities were located inside enclosures, consequently rendering them invisible, this was not always the case. The *triclinium* of Gnaeus Vibrius Saturninus at Pompeii (*22*) could be seen from outside the enclosure and, despite the presence of enclosures in association with several tombs at Isola Sacra, there appears to have been an overwhelming desire to locate *biclinia* in highly public and visible positions *outside* the tombs. This allowed the participants to further display themselves to the wider community. The evidence of Isola Sacra seems to indicate that the community who used the cemetery on a regular basis were making specific statements about their identity. These people, predominantly former slaves, slaves and the lower classes, were all anxious to legitimise their position within society. As previously observed, reclining was itself a sign of status and privilege, and when juxtaposed with the small picnics occurring elsewhere in the cemetery would have made a particularly striking statement.

Despite the opportunities for public display that dining in the cemetery offered, it must also be observed that the activities that took place there centred largely on the family. It was their responsibility to observe the appropriate rites and it would have been members of that family who reclined outside the tomb. This did not necessarily reduce the impact of the image being publicly advertised, and the presence of a united family group may in fact have reinforced it. Indeed, in addition to this process, these occasions created an opportunity for social negotiation of a different kind, between family members and friends, which may subsequently have affected the atmosphere of such events in a similar way to that of dining with the family in the domestic garden. These family-based activities confirmed the identity of members in relation to one another and solidified the bonds and hierarchies that bound them together. Aspects of these occasions may have been necessarily formal due to their religious nature, but the fact that the proceedings directly concerned the family may have lessened its impact. Christian critics of such events describe those taking part as becoming 'boisterously drunk' and the raucous arrival at Trimalchio's dinner party of an inebriated guest who had come directly from a funerary feast and proceeds to enlighten the other guests with descriptions of the food and drink on offer there (Petronius, *Satyricon*, 66) perhaps gives some idea of their relaxed atmosphere. The open-air location of the banquet may have lent a further degree of informality to the proceedings, as has been suggested for domestic dining. This is supported further by the fact that members of burial clubs were required to carry out such rites on behalf of their fellow members. These clubs were concerned equally with burial and companionship, and it is therefore likely that their gatherings were relaxed, informal affairs. When members of Roman society are imagined dining in the environment of the cemetery, it should not be a picture of sombre, formal gatherings, but celebratory meals enjoyed in the company of good friends or close family.

THE GARDEN OF THE LIVING AND THE GARDEN OF THE DEAD

Unfortunately the lack of suitable preservation conditions within the cemeteries of Ostia, Isola Sacra and other areas of Italy prevents a reconstruction of their environment beyond the built structures within them. However, it is important to acknowledge that they originally would not have been as sterile and empty as they can appear today. It was common for tombs to be provided with gardens abounding in flowers, plants, trees, vines and vegetables, the produce of which could be sold in order to raise funds for the maintenance of the tomb or banquets. A satirical poem (to a dead gnat) describes some of the plants and flowers that may have been found within a garden tomb or cemetery:

> Here are to grow acanthus and the blushing rose with crimson bloom, and violets of every kind. Here are Spartan myrtle and hyacinth, and here saffron … soaring laurel … oleander and lilies … rosemary and the Sabine plant … marigold, and glistening ivy … amaranth … and ever-flowering laurestine (Virgil, *Culex* 398-407)

The cemetery environment may therefore have been as luxurious and pleasant as that of the domestic garden in which it was so popular to dine. As a result, those who consumed meals in such surroundings may have made little distinction between domestic and funerary contexts. The relative informality of *al fresco* dining in the garden may have been transferred to the cemetery, especially in light of the fact that both activities focused primarily on close friends and family. The opportunities for display and self promotion that both contexts offered remained a vital part of the activity, but were overshadowed by the relaxed and familial nature of the environment in which they took place and the company in which they dined.

CONCLUSION

Al fresco dining in Roman Italy can be seen to have been about more than a pleasant climate and long summer evenings. Whether diners reclined on the ground or specially built couches, dining out-of-doors lent itself to informality.

This is particularly evident when one examines those participating and when compared with the strict hierarchy and formality of the indoor triclinium. Outdoor dining, whether in the cemetery or at home, was likely to have been more spontaneous than its indoor counterpart, with less concern for order and structure. This is not to say that dining out-of-doors lost all sense of formality. The meals consumed amongst the tombs and monuments of the cemetery took place as part of a specific religious ceremony and in accordance with strict traditions and rites and, as such, may have been far more structured than the evidence allows us to reconstruct. What is more, the creation of permanent dining structures in both domestic and funerary contexts indicates an attempt to make such activities more formal and aligned with respectable practice – it was, after all, always essential to recline. Unlike lavish public banquets or those held within the confines of the indoor dining room, the involvement of the family was paramount to *al fresco* dining and contributed towards an atmosphere of luxury, informality and celebration, even when members of that family were no longer alive.

Emma-Jayne Graham

ACKNOWLEDGEMENTS

I would like to thank Maureen Carroll for her assistance in the preparation of this chapter and for providing several of the illustrations, and Cat Howarth for reading and commenting on an earlier version. *Colour plate 5* and figs *19, 20* and *21* were provided by Maureen Carroll; fig. *22* is after Mau, 1899, fig. 235; fig. *23* is after Floriani Squarciapino, 1958 fig. 47; fig. *24* is after Baldassarre *et al.*, 1996, fig. 31; and the remaining figures are by the author.

BIBLIOGRAPHY

Angelucci, S., Baldassarre, I., Bragantini, I., Lauro, M. G., Mannucci, V., Mazzoleni, A., Morselli, C. and Taglietti, F., 'Sepolture e riti nella necropolis dell'Isola Sacra', *Bollettino di Archeologia*, 5-6 (1990), pp.49-113

Baldassarre, I., Bragantini, I., Morselli, C. and Taglietti, F., *Necropoli Di Porto. Isola Sacra* (Rome, 1996)

Carroll, M., *Earthly Paradises. Ancient Gardens in History and Archaeology* (London, 2003)

Dunbabin, K.M.D., 'Triclinium and Stibadium', in W.J. Slater (ed.), *Dining in a Classical Context* (Ann Arbor, 1991), pp.121-148

Dunbabin, K.M.D., *The Roman Banquet. Images of Conviviality* (Cambridge, 2003)

Ellis, S.P., *Roman Housing* (London, 2000)

Farrar, L., *Ancient Roman Gardens* (Stroud, 2000)

Floriani Squarciapino, M., *Scavi Di Ostia III. Le Necropoli* (Rome, 1958)

Hopkins, K., *Death and Renewal* (Cambridge, 1983)

Jashemski, W.F., *The Gardens of Pompeii, Herculaneum and the Villas Destroyed by Vesuvius* (New York, 1979)

Purcell, N., 'Town in country and country in town', in E.B. MacDougall (ed.), *Ancient Roman Villa Gardens* (Washington DC, 1987), pp.185-203

— , 'The Roman garden as a domestic building', in I.M. Barton (ed.), *Roman Domestic Buildings* (Exeter, 1996), pp.121-151

Ricotti, E.S.P., 'The importance of water in Roman garden triclinia', in E.B. MacDougall (ed.), *Ancient Roman Villa Gardens* (Washington DC, 1987), pp.135-184

Thébert, Y., 'Private life and domestic architecture in Roman Africa', in P. Veyne (ed.), *A History of Private Life. 1. From Pagan Rome to Byzantium* (London, 1987), pp.313-409

five

HANSEATIC TABLE CULTURE IN NORTHERN EUROPE 1200-1600: THE ARCHAEOLOGY OF CULTURAL TRANSFER AND RESISTANCE

This chapter extracts some results and key themes generated by an archaeological survey of the Hanseatic ceramic market in the Baltic between *c.*1200 and 1600. The distribution of excavated household ceramic wares from over 3,000 discrete assemblages from 67 individual sites forms an index of commercial contacts, as well as technological and cultural transfer, from western Europe to Scandinavia, Fennoscandia and the eastern Baltic region. In addition to its value as a guide to trading activity, the ceramic evidence also provides a physical measure of the spread and adoption of Hanseatic domestic *habitus* (or lifestyle as reflected, for example, in dining practices, recreational activities and in the layout and decoration of living spaces), particularly in the spheres of dining ritual and the interior environment. In view of their short lifespan and survival in the ground, imported ceramics and their contexts have the potential to provide a quantitative index of cultural transfer to the region over time and space. This transfer may be manifested in the form of *horizontal* commercial or social links between urban, mercantile communities in the North Sea and Baltic regions. Comparative analysis of urban and castle assemblages, which may contain certain luxury imports, such as stoneware vessels, Mediterranean maiolica or relief-moulded stove-tiles, injects a vital *vertical* dimension into the equation, their qualitative attributes helping to establish elite patterns of consumption and social competition in the marketplace.

The shifting distributions of forms, designs and iconography in the domestic ceramic market of the Baltic over the period of study form a guide to the penetration of new technologies and fashions, together with religious and political loyalties, into the homes of the region's urban merchant communities and residential feudal elite, many of whom were living on the very edge of the European cultural orbit. In this context the remote Hanseatic *Kontor* (trading post) of Novgorod, situated on the edge of the Russian pine forest zone, forms a case study in the archaeology of cultural resistance. Here, despite the 'Hanseatic' signature of the range of imports excavated in the centre of the city, the relatively polarised distribution of western ceramics around the alien mercantile enclave contrasts strikingly with patterns recorded in nearby trading centres on the Livonian-Russian frontier, where western imports circulated more widely amongst the host community. Clearly in Novgorod, with its domestic wood culture, there was entrenched resistance to the use of highly decorated ceramic tableware from the West, irrespective of its technological superiority.

THE HANSA IN THE BALTIC: COMMERCIAL AND CULTURAL NETWORKS

The Hansa formed the principal agent of trade and exchange in northern Europe and the Baltic during the medieval to early modern period. The origin of this confederation of German cities can be traced back to the foundation of Lübeck (Germany) in 1158. In the wake of conquest by the Teutonic Order, German merchants rapidly colonised the lands to the east during the course of the following century and founded such towns as Rostock, Stralsund (Germany), Danzig (now Gdańsk, Poland) and Riga (Latvia). Hanseatic trade reached its zenith during the fourteenth to fifteenth centuries with the foundation of permanent trading posts or *Kontore* at Novgorod in the east, Bergen (Norway) in the north, and London and Bruges (Belgium) in the west. Together they formed a dynamic economic and cultural network, which stretched the length and breadth of Europe and beyond.

The Hanseatic trading system which had emerged by the late thirteenth century drew the west, the east and the north of the Continent together by acting as an intermediary for the exchange of goods between two very different patterns of production: raw materials from the east and finished/semi-finished products from the west, and by stimulating the wider long-distance market. Despite their dispersed geographical position, a new type of ship, the cog, which developed around 1200, enabled the Hanseatic merchants to maintain economic superiority over the Continent for centuries. It was more capacious and more stable than previous models, and at around 200-300 tons, could carry two to three times the cargo. The movement of raw and processed material and finished goods inevitably also necessitated the to and fro of people. In addition to traders, wholesalers and retailers, members of the aristocracy, administrators, soldiers, churchmen and, crucially, craftsmen – shipbuilders, altarpiece-carvers and potters – were prepared to migrate long distances, with the prospect of exploiting new markets for their products. Thus, perhaps as influential as the growing economic and technological dominance of the Hanseatic League, were the 'horizontal' cultural networks, which developed between trading partners, towns and families the length and breadth of the Baltic region.

Hanseatic urban settlements in northern Europe shared many things in common, not only in their commercial function, but also in their language and in their cultural, religious and political identity. Art-historians have spoken in defining terms of a cosmopolitan Hanseatic 'signature' which was articulated physically through a shared vocabulary of town plan, public building, church layout (designed as much for business meetings as for the veneration of the Saints), a distinctive architectural style of brick step-gabled buildings (*Backsteingotik*), and through common design in the visual arts, particularly in the ecclesiastical and devotional spheres. Here carved and painted altarpieces endowed by leading merchant families or guilds, carved bench- and pew-ends, monumental grave slabs and baptismal fonts and doors in cast bronze all allude to the shared religious and social values of the urban bourgeois elite.

THE BALTIC CERAMIC MARKET, c. 1200–1600

So little of the Hansa's traditional historiography has been concerned with the routines of everyday life and material expression in the home. Where this question of domestic comfort in the Hanseatic household has been considered, the emphasis has inevitably been restricted to random museum survivals of precious and base-metalware, textiles or furniture. However, urban excavation in advance of city-centre redevelopment – particularly in the eastern Baltic zone since the fall of the Iron Curtain – has provided the opportunity to adjust this asymmetrical narrative. The wealth and diversity of the archaeological record generated by Baltic towns and castles are reflected in the rich ceramic sample (*26*). With their short lifespan, ubiquity on the ground and distribution across diverse social contexts, ceramics can be cross-examined as *Kulturträger* in their own right alongside gabled brick architecture and ecclesiastical objects.

A further important development in recent years has been the controlled excavation of a series of harbour and shipwreck assemblages of cargoes of western European ceramics around the mouth of the Baltic at the Öresund, along the coastal archipelago of Finland, and along the coast of Mecklenburg-Lower Pomerania. These new finds are beginning to reveal a clearer picture of

26 Selection of highly decorated red earthenwares and imported German proto- and full stonewares excavated during drainage of the harbour of the castle and town at Kalmar, S.E. Sweden, in 1933/34. Thirteenth- to early fourteenth-century date

the process of transhipment at major ports and extensive coastal redistribution along the Baltic littoral by the smaller carrying trade.

While it is unrealistic to reconstruct the incomings and outgoings of long-distance commodity trade on the basis of pottery sherds, the analysis of traded domestic wares provides a measure of cultural contacts between regions, particularly in the sphere of domestic *habitus*. In contrast to the documentary record of international trade links in the Baltic, it is through the excavated record that we are able to more clearly quantify the degree to which Hanseatic 'lifestyles' penetrated expatriate mercantile communities across the region – and, crucially through inter-site analysis, at what social level. Archaeological collections from castle sites form a measure of quality control for the study of urban mercantile consumption and vertical transfer in the market.

RED EARTHENWARE AND STONEWARE: THE EMERGENCE OF A COMMON MARKET

The early phases of the emerging international pottery market in the Baltic during the thirteenth to fourteenth centuries are dominated by the migration of red earthenware production from western Europe to the southern Baltic zone and by the increasing competition between the highly decorated redwares and the technologically superior stonewares from western and northern Germany.

The development of towns along the Baltic littoral during the course of the thirteenth century stimulated a demand for high-quality ceramic tableware suited to the needs of urban living and social competition. Initially imports of highly decorated lead-glazed redwares from the North Sea coast of Flanders and the Netherlands satisfied the demand at the expense of imports from England or western France: the Bruges kilns of around 1200-1350 acting as epicentre of the industry. But within a decade or so of the Bruges industry beginning, all the major towns of the Low Countries supported a redware manufacture which continued until *c.*1275 as archaeological discoveries at Aardenburg, Haarlem, Utrecht, Leiden, Bergen-op-Zoom, Dordrecht, Breda and Delft have recently demonstrated. Although attached to individual urban economies, the industry was clearly a homogeneous one, the technological uniformity and narrow repertoire in terms of typology and ornament suggestive of close workshop links. But the discovery of a series of redware production centres along the Öresund spanning the Danish islands of Funen and Zealand and the coastline of western Scania, at Lübeck and more recently at sites along the Mecklenburg coast, producing typologically and technologically indistinguishable wares to the Low Countries exports, suggests the movement of western European workshops into the southern Baltic region. Here suitable clays were ubiquitous, and could be fired through the oxidising process to emulate the red earthenware jugs and cooking utensils, such as dripping pans, so familiar to the urban populations of the North Sea littoral.

A distinguishing feature of the southern Baltic redware rod-handled jugs of the mid-thirteenth to mid-fourteenth centuries is the plastic decoration in a white-firing clay with a copper or iron-rich lead glaze, the most common forms being notch-rouletted zones or bands and applied strips (sometimes rouletted) forming vertical panels or large chevrons filled with fish scales, leaf designs or individual pellets, rosettes or raspberry motifs. Occasionally the upper bodies and necks of these jugs are applied with anthropomorphic decoration, the so-called hooded 'monk's face' being the most common.

The distribution of western European and regionally produced redwares stretches from the mouth of the Baltic in the south to Finland and Novgorod

27 Fire-damaged lead-glazed redware jug applied with enigmatic human figures (with 'monk faces') around the neck and body. Found during excavation at the extra-mural settlement associated with the Episcopal castle at Lihula, Estonia, founded with assistance of the Teutonic Order in 1238. Second half of the thirteenth century, probably made in the southern Baltic region in Russia to the north. Their relatively low proportional representation on town sites along the Mecklenburg and Pomeranian coastline during the thirteenth century suggests that these wares enjoyed a certain social premium which made them only accessible to the Hanseatic mercantile and rural feudal elite. At Kołobzreg (Poland, formerly Kolberg) highly decorated redwares account for between four and seven per cent of all table ceramics used in the port between the mid-thirteenth and early fourteenth centuries.

Castle sites around the Baltic Sea region have produced some of the largest and more ornate groups of redware anthropomorphic jugs. Early twentieth-century excavations at the Danish royal castle of Skanör, located on the Falsterbo peninsula of Scania guarding the entrance to the Öresund, is the source of a substantial and varied assemblage including several face-jug fragments. More spectacular still is the recent find of an almost complete anthropomorphic jug from a substantial house just to the south of the outer bailey of the episcopal castle of Lihula in north-west Estonia which was built after 1238 with the support of Teutonic Order. Although heavily burnt in a fire it is possible to make out that the vessel is applied around the body with full-length clerics, saints or possibly female figures in long robes (27). Their faces, moulded inside hoods and surmounted by headdresses or halos, are emphasised in high relief between the creases of the vessel's folded neck. Excavations at the castle during the 1980s-'90s have also produced a substantial assemblage of other imported ceramics of the thirteenth to sixteenth centuries, including further pieces of South Baltic redware and proto- and fully fused stonewares from Rhenish and Lower Saxon production centres. The range of imports found at Lihula compares closely to the Hanseatic urban ceramic profile of Estonia, where a similar range of imported wares has been identified in Tallinn, Tartu, Pärnu and Haapsalu. On one level the ceramic profile of the castle conforms to the Hanseatic urban consumer pattern in the Baltic with its range of imported wares yet, on another, its social ranking is emphasised by the presence of such highly decorated vessels.

In terms of numbers, however, the late medieval international ceramic trade in the Baltic is dominated by the competition between stoneware producers based in the central Rhineland, Lower Saxony and in Saxony. Although outcrops of clay suitable for high temperature stoneware production were limited to Germany, its robust body enabled stoneware to be transported in bulk and over long distances. Following transhipping at major ports, finds of wrecks containing cargoes of medieval German stoneware in the archipelago off south-western Finland provides a model for the process of coastal redistribution of stoneware in the Baltic zone. The continuing work at the Nauvo wreck by researchers attached to the National Maritime Museum of Finland has produced over 30 contemporaneous decanting and drinking vessels dating to the early fourteenth century, all originating from a single stoneware factory source in Lower Saxony. Possibly unloaded at Stockholm, the vessels probably formed part of a small cargo of Western domestic utensils heading for the nearby Hanseatic trading port of Turku (Åbo) (Finland).

Intensive workshop production resulted in a relatively low cost to the consumer and the ability to reach a wide spectrum of the population. The rapid development of the fully fused stoneware body fired to between 1200 and 1400°c (with a porosity value of 0.4 per cent) in the Rhineland and Lower Saxony at the beginning of the fourteenth century coincides with and may even be consequential on the growth of urban populations in northern Europe. With its technologically superior body, which is impervious to liquids, stainless and odour free, stoneware revolutionised so many domestic activities from washing-up to preserving food. In addition, its increasingly varied repertoire of forms over the fourteenth to fifteenth centuries reflects a market response to the multiple drinking, decanting, transport, storage and sanitary needs of town dwellers and castle communities across the Continent (28). By 1350 the highly decorated redwares had begun take a lower profile in the Baltic market due to the pressure from German stoneware exports. Despite the plain, utilitarian body, stoneware captured a niche in the popular tableware market of northern Europe, enabling the aspiring middle classes to imitate aristocratic drinking and dining practices in a less expensive medium, substituting precious or base metalware and drinking glasses with a finely potted ceramic that imitated their role (*colour plate 7*). In view of its wide penetration of the international domestic ceramics market, German stoneware may be regarded as a type-fossil of mercantile or 'Hanseatic' urban culture, a unique class of *Kulturträger*, which linked consumers irrespective of means from London to Tallinn and beyond.

Finds from the castle harbour (Slottsfjärden) at Kalmar in southern Sweden provide an instant synopsis of competition in the Baltic stoneware market over the late medieval period (26). Out of the 885 German stoneware vessels of fourteenth- to fifteenth-century date, 68 per cent could be sourced to Siegburg (Rhineland), 21 per cent to Lower Saxony, 9 per cent to Waldenburg (Saxony), and 3 per cent to Langerwehe and Raeren, and others in the Rhineland. In addition to the associated social status afforded by its castle, the concentrations of German stoneware found at Kalmar, which make up around 5 per cent of the overall domestic ceramic inventory from the town, may also be explained by the relatively high numbers of alien names recorded as resident in the city. During the late fourteenth century, for instance, one third out of a total of 2,000 family names listed as resident in the city were German in origin. A similar explanation could also be made for the Stockholm stoneware sequence. Here the well-documented population of resident German merchants provides a context

28 Jacobakanne drinking jugs from Waldenburg, Saxony, excavated at the Danish royal castle of Skanör on the Falsterbo peninsula, Scania, Sweden, which was abandoned, *c.* 1425

for the high frequency of imported stoneware finds recorded in the Gamla Stan (Old Town) and in neighbouring districts.

Among the bulk trade in German stoneware to the Baltic during the late Middle Ages there is one group of vessels, however, which, by virtue of its elaborate ornament and biased social distribution, can be discussed realistically in terms of a status indicator. According to recent trace-elemental analysis of the ceramic body, the Lausitz region of Saxony is the most likely source for a series of high-quality stoneware goblets and beakers of fifteenth-century date found across the study zone (*29*). These characteristically dark-bodied and thinly-potted stonewares with their ecclesiastical forms, painted anthropomorphic plastic ornament, intricate geometric rouletting and applied gold foil surfaces are found in small quantities but enjoy a widespread distribution from the Öresund to western Finland and Estonia. Apart from a limited number of finds from the mercantile waterfront and mercantile residential districts of Stockholm and Turku, the middle to northern Baltic finds of this ornate group of stoneware drinking vessels are exclusive to castle and monastic sites. To name but two examples, excavations in the 1920s and in the mid-1990s in the courtyard of Stockholm

29 Stoneware goblets from the Lausitz in Saxony: left with applied female head, and right with geometric chequer-board rouletting and triangular stamps filled with gold foil. Fifteenth century. Found on the site of the Riddarhuset, Riddarholmen, and on the Skeppsbron waterfront respectively

castle have produced fragments of three cylindrical chequer-rouletted goblets, while in 1987 a goblet fragment with the same chequer-board surface design was recovered from the outer bailey of the Bishop of Finland's castle and residence at Kuusisto, western Finland (c. 1318-1528). On the eastern Baltic coast a group of goblets recovered from the 1531 destruction levels at the Dominican monastery of St Catherine in Tallinn's lower town further emphasises the social premium of this particular Hanseatic trade good.

Archaeological finds have also demonstrated the extent to which utilitarian plain stoneware vessels were valued among those expatriate communities situated on the very margins of European cultural contact. Excavations on St James's Street in the Livonian frontier town of Tartu (Estonia), have produced an example of a standard fifteenth-century Siegburg beaker inside its original moulded leather container which was incised with a frieze of forest animals and birds. A further discovery at Greifswald on the Mecklenburg-Lower Pomerania coast of an early fifteenth-century Siegburg stoneware beaker encased within a tooled leather cover, reinforces the impression that, despite the ubiquity of western European stoneware in the region, such vessels were highly prized and their value could be enhanced through embellishment with another medium more suitable for decoration, in this case moulded and tooled leather.

RELIEF–MOULDED STONEWARE AND POLYCHROME TIN–GLAZED EARTHENWARE: THE ARRIVAL OF THE CONTINENTAL RENAISSANCE

The second phase of the Hanseatic pottery market in the Baltic is characterised by a shift in the balance between the utilitarian and social roles of traded ceramic tableware at the start of the sixteenth century. Decorated stoneware, transformed by the development of moulded relief technology, and the introduction of polychrome-painted tin-glazed earthenware (maiolica) from southern and western Europe, injected a new luxury element based on the latest western European popular taste and a greater degree of social competition into the Baltic marketplace.

The co-terminus introduction of applied relief moulded ornament based on contemporary printed designs and salt glazing designed to emphasise the reliefs marked a profound shift in the function and social role of German stoneware at the beginning of the sixteenth century. These innovations gave the medium a radically new dimension: glazed relief ornament enabled stoneware to compete for the first time in terms of looks as well as function in the dining sphere, particularly with metal vessels and decorated glassware. Stoneware manufacturers drew on a wide range of contemporary popular design sources, especially those of the fashionable *Kleinmeister* engraver-artists, which could be reproduced at a minimal cost through mould technology. Stoneware rose rapidly in status and retail cost. It was bought by the nobility, the Church and the urban merchant class. It employed, besides a wide spectrum of mythological and biblical figures and scenes (*30*), allegorical personifications, coats-of-arms and Antique heroes, the explicitly political and ideological imagery emerging in contemporary Reformation Germany. Unlike Italian or Netherlandish maiolica, which are characterised by individually hand-painted ornament, stoneware potters could replicate complex products in bulk.

The growing social premium attached to stoneware can be observed in its biased archaeological distribution towards castle and elite residential sites across the Baltic region. Few stratified sixteenth-century phases are without their Renaissance stoneware assemblage, some more varied and richer than others. The Danish castles of Scania are particularly representative, the royal

30 Frechen stoneware *Schnelle* tankard applied with scenes from the Temptation. Excavated in the Rundeln quarter of Malmö, southern Sweden. Mid-sixteenth century

residences of Lindholmen, Malmöhus and the baronial castles of Glimmingehus and Krapperup being most prolific in terms of excavated finds. The finds of Cologne Schnelle and Pinte tankards with applied Renaissance-style allegorical and foliate ornament represent the upper end of the stoneware retail market and suggest a high degree of fashion consciousness in the drinking culture of the castle household. The recent find from the north Bailey of Riga Castle, the headquarters of the Livonian Order, of a Cologne Schnelle tankard of around 1535-50, applied with female allegorical figures of Anger, Envy and Guilt, places the post-Dissolution secular inhabitants of the castle into the centre of the contemporary European cultural matrix.

In contrast to stoneware, tin-glazed earthenwares were a rare commodity in the Baltic Sea region until the late fifteenth century, when the introduction of industrial production in the Southern Netherlands provided a closer source of luxury table ceramics to the Hanseatic trading towns of the North. Until this point tin-glazed lustreware vessels from Iberia accounted for the majority of maiolica imports circulating in the region. Spanish lustreware vessels from Malaga and Valencia have now been identified in fourteenth- to early sixteenth-century levels on urban sites around the Baltic rim. The impression of social premium attached to these wares is reinforced by the survival of a near-complete Late Valencian Overall Lustre lugged bowl of the late fifteenth to early sixteenth century found in the moat of Glimmingehus, eastern Scania, during the mid-1930s. The castle was rebuilt in stone as the mainland residence for the Danish nobleman, Jens Helgersen Ulfstrand, Governor of Gotland, and is dated by its dedication stone to 1499.

Polychrome maiolica ceramics increased in their regional market share throughout the course of the sixteenth to early seventeenth centuries, as Italy replaced Spain as the major supply source. Although still relatively low in terms of overall numbers, Ligurian, Montelupo and Faenza White maiolicas enjoyed a widespread distribution in Hanseatic ports around the Baltic rim. Excavations in major mercantile centres such as Elblag (Elbing) in Poland and Stockholm, Kalmar, Malmö and Lund in Sweden have produced the most substantial groups, their elevated social contexts emphasising the increasing stratification of the local domestic pottery market. The arrival of the first Netherlandish maiolica imports in the Baltic around 1500 coincides to a large degree with the demise of the Hanseatic monopoly of the household commodities trade in the region and the increasing influence of the Low Countries. However, the archaeological distribution map of the earliest Italo-Netherlandish maiolicas in the region is dominated by urban centres, as illustrated by assemblages from Lübeck, Copenhagen and Rostock. The finds reveal the dependence on embedded Hanseatic trading networks for these new products. Meanwhile, a sample of castle finds emphasises the social premium and cultural consciousness attached to these multi-coloured finewares. The deposit of polychrome albarelli (drug jars) excavated in 1939 at the Swedish royal castle at Turku (Åbo) in south-west Finland, which can be dated to the first half of the sixteenth century on the basis of their context association, may represent the existence of a castle pharmacy on the western European model.

Following the pattern in the English Channel and the North Sea, the mid- to late sixteenth century imported tin-glazed earthenware spectrum is dominated by the 'Malling' wares. These mottled polychrome-glazed earthenware jugs, mugs and bottles have now been chemically sourced to Antwerp. Their archaeological distribution is characterised by a concentration in the southern Baltic, notably along the North German Baltic coast at Greifswald, Rostock and Lüneburg and also in the Hanseatic trading towns of Copenhagen, Malmö and Kalmar which flank the entrance to the Baltic. Finds of Malling jugs and mugs on castle sites in Sweden, including the courtyard of Stockholm Castle, the Danish aristocratic residences of Krapperup, Scania, Glimmingehus, and the episcopal and – from the mid-sixteenth century – royal castle of Kronoberg, near Växjö, Småland, inject a vertical dimension into the distribution pattern.

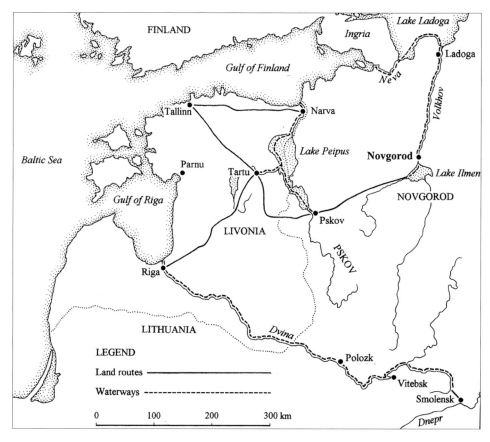

31 Map showing Novgorod in relation to the north-east Baltic with water-borne and overland trade routes from the Gulf of Finland and from Hanseatic towns in Livonia

POSTSCRIPT: HANSEATIC CULTURAL TRANSFER AND RESISTANCE

In the case of Novgorod, however, located out on the north-eastern frontier of the Hanseatic cultural zone, the pattern of urban distribution of western tableware ceramics appears atypical (*31*). This principal Hanseatic trading station (*Kontor*) situated at the northern end of the Baltic-Black Sea and Baltic-Caspian trade routes, supported two substantial European mercantile communities during the late Middle Ages, firstly the Gotlanders' Court or *Gotenhof* founded by the early twelfth century, and secondly the Court of St Peter, or *St Peterhof*, the German trading enclave firmly established in 1191. Both settlements clustered close to the wharfs of the River Volkhov on the market side of the city. The primary purpose of these trading stations was to exploit the rich forest wilderness of northern Russia and Karelia for pelts, pine resin (for distilling into pitch) and honey. In return, the city of Novgorod consumed vital raw materials such as amber and silver from the Baltic and finished goods from western Europe, including cloth, metal utensils along with foodstuffs and preservatives, including herring and salt.

With their short lifespan and survival in the ground, imported ceramics and their spatial distributions have the potential to provide a concrete and quantifiable measure of the penetration of western or 'Hanseatic' lifestyles among the host community, notably in the dining sphere. In actuality, however, the relatively polarised distribution of western ceramic imports around the alien residential areas of the city contrasts strikingly with the pattern recorded in other regional trading centres, notably in the neighbouring Livonian-Russian border city of Pskov where western imports were dispersed more widely around the settlement

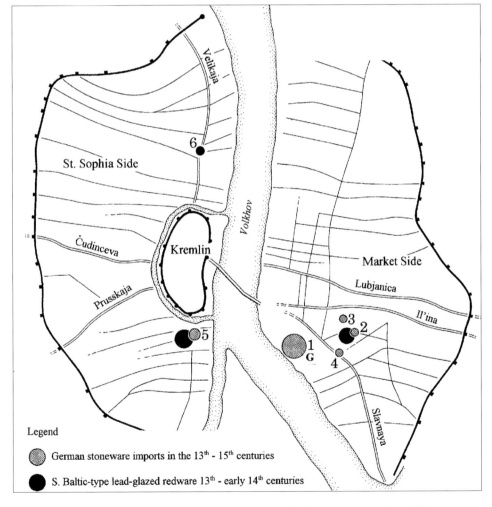

32 Plan of medieval Novgorod showing the distribution and relative concentrations of German stoneware and South Baltic redware

(*32*). Evidently in Novgorod, with its strong domestic wood culture, there was entrenched resistance to the use of ceramic tableware from the West.

Although technically superior in their impervious, stain-free and odourless body, imported stonewares, together with decorative lead-glazed red earthenwares, were generally rejected by the native population in favour of wooden drinking vessels. Here, on the edge of the pine forest zone, pottery (in this case reduced grey earthenware) was largely relegated to the utilitarian functions of cooking and food preparation while wood, with its suitability for lathe-turning, carved decoration and painted surfaces, was more suited to table use. This preference for wood at the expense of ceramics for dining, therefore, is not just a functional, but a cultural equation. The outcome reveals strongly embedded resistance among the majority of the native population to alien social practices. The asymmetrical imported pottery distribution visible in Novgorod contrasts starkly with the picture from contemporary Hanseatic *Kontor* sites such as London or Bruges, where Rhenish stoneware imports are found across the urban landscape, irrespective of social or functional topography. Here in Novgorod, on the edge of the forest zone and behind the Christian-Orthodox frontier of northern Europe, both alien mercantile and native host communities were keen to express their respective ethnic identities and cultural loyalties, through their own material culture, including, and most visibly, in the dining sphere.

CONCLUSION

Imported western ceramics fulfilled dual utilitarian and social roles among the medieval to early modern mercantile communities living in the Baltic Sea region. Beyond relics of complex distance trading mechanisms, their archaeological distributions provide a measure of the absorption of Hanseatic cultural codes and lifestyle practices, notably in the spheres of dining culture and domestic comfort. The study of individual luxury products and the composition of assemblages from high-status residential sites, such as castles, inject a vertical dimension into the analysis. The success of these commodities hints at something more than long-distance commercial transactions and the transfer of technical expertise. Rather, the patterns of consumption identified reflect a brand loyalty element and a measure of the embedded cultural and possibly ethnic motivations, which characterise the Hanseatic mercantile communities on the Baltic rim.

In a phrase, the ceramic evidence emerging in the Baltic zone of the late medieval to early modern period points to a proto-colonial scenario comparable to early European contact sites in North America and the Caribbean where settlers asserted their cultural affiliations, ethnicity, class and religion through the active use of domestic goods and the transfer of craft production to new markets. In the case of Novgorod, isolated territorially beyond the edge of European cultural influence, there were social obstacles to the use of imported table ceramics, which remained largely the preserve of itinerant Western merchants. Highly decorated redwares and high-fired stonewares appear to have been actively rejected by the indigenous population who, despite the technological superiority of the imports, remained loyal to its highly refined painted wood tableware culture.

David Gaimster

ACKNOWLEDGEMENTS

The research on which this paper is based has been sponsored by the Swedish Institute, British Academy, Society of Antiquaries of London, the Nordenstedt Foundation, Sweden, and the AHRB Research Exchange Scheme. The work at Novgorod over three years (1997-99) was supported by INTAS (International Association for the promotion of co-operation with scientists from the New Independent States of the former Soviet Union). The study of the trade in western European ceramic tableware to the Baltic follows a previous analysis of the Hanseatic pottery market in the English Channel and North Sea zones, with London as its focus. Illustrations are reproduced courtesy of the following museum: Statens Historiska Museer, Stockholm, and Kalmar Läns Museum (fig. *26*); Estonian History Museum, Tallinn (inv. AMK 583:150) (fig. *27*); Lund University Historical Museum (inv. LUHM 17300:XII) (fig. *28*); and Stockholms Stadsmuseum (inv. SSM 7531 and 170.704) (fig. *29*); Malmö Museer (inv. 5827) (fig. *30*). Figures *31* and *32* were drawn by Jim Farrant of the British Museum. *Colour plate 7* is reproduced by permission of Wallraf-Richartz Museum, Cologne (inv. WRM 471).

BIBLIOGRAPHY

Falk, A. and Gaimster, D., 'Maiolica in the Baltic c.1350-1650: a material index of Hanseatic trade and cultural exchange', in J. Veeckman (ed.), *Majolica en glas: van Italië naar Antwerpen en verder. De overdracht van technologie in de 16de- begin 17de eeuw*, Stad Antwerpen, afdeling archeologie (Antwerp, 2002), pp.371-390

Gaimster, D., 'Cross-Channel ceramic trade in the late Middle Ages: archaeological evidence for the spread of Hanseatic culture to Britain', in M. Gläser (ed.),

Archäologie des Mittelalters und Bauforschung im Hanseraum. Eine Festschrift für Günter Fehring, Schriften des Kulturhistorischen Museums in Rostock (Rostock, 1993), pp.251-260

— , *German Stoneware 1200-1900. Archaeology and Cultural History* (London, 1997)

— , 'The Baltic ceramic market c.1200-1600: an archaeology of the Hansa', *Fennoscandia Archaeologica*, 16 (1999), pp.59-69

— , 'German stoneware and stove-tiles: type-fossils of Hanseatic culture in the Baltic c.1200-1600', in R. Vissak and A. Mäesalu (eds), *The Medieval Town in the Baltic. Hanseatic History and Archaeology*, Proceedings of the first and second seminar, Tartu, Estonia, 6th-7th June 1997 and 26th-27th June 1998 (Tartu, 1999), pp.53-64

— , 'Hansaeatic trade and cultural exchange in the Baltic c.1200-1600: pottery from wrecks and harbours', in H. von Schmettow et al. (eds), *Schutz des Kulturerbes unter Wasser*, Beiträge zum Internationalen Kongress für Unterwasserarchäologie (IKUWA '99), Sassnitz auf Rügen (Lübstorf, 2000), pp.237-247

— , 'Pelts, pitch and pottery. The archaeology of Hanseatic trade in medieval Novgorod', in M. Brisbane & D. Gaimster (eds), *Novgorod: The Archaeology of the Russian Medieval City and its Hinterland*, British Museum Occasional Paper, 141 (London, 2001), pp.67-78

— , 'Life and lifestyle in the Baltic castle: patterns in ceramic consumption c.1200-1600', in J. Skaarup *et al.* (eds), *Castella Maris Baltici* V, Langelands Museum/Nationalmuseet (Rudkøbing, 2001), pp.51-66

— , *The Baltic Ceramic Market 1200-1600: Hanseatic Trade and Cultural Transfer* (Oxford, forthcoming)

Rebkowski, M., 'Medieval glazed pottery imported into Pomerania. A survey of the present state of research', in A. Buko and W. Pela (eds), *Imported and Locally Produced Pottery: Methods of Identification and Analysis*, Scientific Society of Polish Archaeologists, Department of Warsaw (Warsaw, 1997), pp.97-110

Schäfer, H., 'Zur Keramik des 13. und 15. Jahrhunderts in Mecklenburg-Vorpommern', *Bodendenkmalpflege in Mecklenburg-Vorpommern*, 44 (1996), pp.297-335

Stephan, H-G., 'Deutsche Keramik im Handelsraum der Hanse', in G. Wiegelmann and R-E. Mohrmann (eds), *Nahrung und Tischkultur im Hanseraum*, Münster (New York, 1996), pp.95-123

Stephan, H.G. and Gaimster, D., 'Die "Falke-Gruppe": Das reich verzierte Lausitzer Steinzeug der Gotik und sein archäologisch-historisches Umfeld', *Zeitschrift für Archäologie des Mittelalters*, 30 (2002), pp.107-163

Verhaeghe, F., 'Medieval and later social networks. The contribution of archaeology', in H. Hundsbichler et al. (eds), *Die Vielfalt der Dinge. Neue Wege zur Analyse mittelalterlicher Sachkultur,* Internationaler Kongress Krems an der Donau Oktober 1997, Forschungen des Instituts für Realienkunde des Mittelalters und der Frühen Neuzeit (Vienna, 1998), pp.263-312

six

POTTERY AND MANNERS

When you have washed your hands, you should touch nothing but what you will be eating. Don't immediately gobble up your bread, rather wait for the first course to be served. It is not proper to cram such large chunks into one's mouth that bits fall right and left; this amounts to boorishness and gluttony. Chew your food thoroughly before swallowing it, for fear of choking yourself. If you don't want to drink like a churl, make sure your mouth is free of food; only the peasant makes such sops in his mouth. And be aware that it is boorish to speak with a full mouth … Do not reach to the bowl in front of your neighbour to take a morsel that seems better than what you have in front of you: that is churlishness. After eating, ask for hand-water, for that is required by medical teaching and it is the decent and easy thing to do.

The above passage, translated from a twelfth-century treatise 'Training for a Gentleman' by Petrus Alphonsi, gives advice that typifies the importance placed on gentility throughout the later medieval period. Alphonsi's work, together with many others in similar vein, demonstrates an enthusiasm for courtly behaviour and emphasizes the ceremonial nature of medieval society, at least at the higher reaches. This chapter is concerned with the archaeological evidence for the ceremony and concentrates on pottery, perhaps the most common artefact recovered from medieval excavations. It is through such a study that the relationships between material culture and social behaviour can be explored and the relationship between archaeological evidence and written history enhanced. The basis of this chapter is the pottery recovered from nine excavations carried out within the walled town of Southampton (Hants), one of the most important ports in medieval England.

This assemblage will be examined in order to discover what pottery can tell us about dining habits and customs in the post-Conquest medieval period. Most specifically this is an analysis of tableware from the twelfth century to around 1520 with subsequent conclusions based on documentary evidence.

Pottery from the post-Conquest medieval period in Southampton can be placed into one of three ceramic periods. The Anglo-Norman period dates from around 1070 to 1250, although most of the pottery found relates to the latter half. The high medieval period dates from around 1250 to 1350 and represents the apex of English medieval ceramic achievement, while the late medieval period covers around 1350 to 1520, but archaeological deposits from the first 80 years or so are scarce and most of the pottery found dates from after about 1450. Examples of pots from all these periods are illustrated, and referenced in the text by the figure number and individual pot number given within parentheses. Further illustrated examples and detailed descriptions may be found in my monograph on the pottery from medieval Southampton. (Brown 2002)

THE ANGLO-NORMAN PERIOD

Both before and after the Norman conquest of England the range of pottery forms is limited and most of it seems to have been made for use either for food storage or preparation (Brown 1995). Figure *33* shows the relative percentages of different types of pottery vessel in use in the Anglo-Norman period. The most common ceramic vessel is the earthenware jar or cooking pot, which represents over 84 per cent of the total weight of sherds recovered. This vessel is, typically, a handbuilt, unglazed form with a rounded base and everted rim (35 (1)), probably made very locally; if not within then close to Southampton. Many examples have sooting on the external surface, which indicates that they have been used in cooking, and this is likely to have been their most common function. Jugs represent the second most common vessel type in the Anglo-Norman assemblage, at 9.5 per cent of the total sherd weight. Locally made jugs or tripod pitchers (35 (4)) were, like jars, handbuilt and coarse in aspect, usually with a rudimentary glaze. Jugs were also imported from Normandy during this period, and these are all wheelthrown, with consistent glazing, and include highly decorated examples such as Rouen-type ware (35 (2, 3)). Just as the jar form is usually identified as a cooking pot so jugs may be characterised as vessels intended for use at table. This is most likely to be true of the Normandy types and it may therefore be likely that the local product, although to our eyes inferior, was used in the same ways. Bowls comprise less than 0.5 per cent of the total Anglo-Norman assemblage,

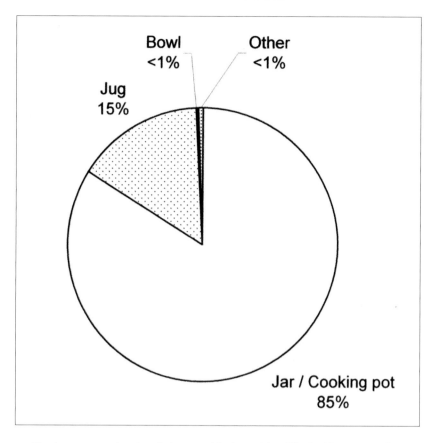

33 Pie chart representing the relative quantities by weight of Anglo-Norman vessel types shown in Table 1

	Rim Percent	Weight (g)	Sherd Count
Jar / Cooking pot	5031	82148	4371
Jug	605	14866	680
Bowl	122	397	15
Other	207	463	20
Unidentified	216	19283	2177
Totals	1150	35009	2892

34 Table 1. Quantities of vessel types in the Anglo-Norman period from nine sites in Southampton

35 Anglo-Norman pottery. 1: Scratch-marked jar/cooking pot; 2: green-glazed Rouen-type jug; 3: red slip-decorated Rouen-type jug; 4: local tripod pitcher

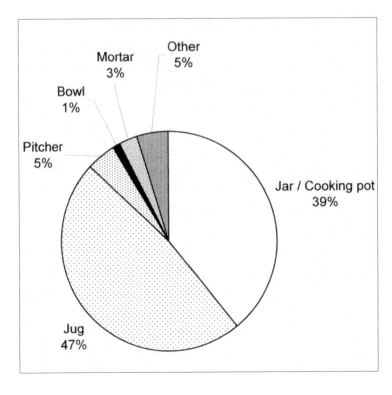

36 Pie chart representing the relative quantities by weight of high medieval vessel types shown in Table 2

by weight. These are made in the same coarseware fabrics as the jars and it is therefore unlikely that they were made for use at table. Lamps comprise the remaining 0.5 per cent of the material quantified in figure *33*.

Documentary sources for this period are rare. The Bayeux tapestry shows the feast that followed William the Conqueror's landing at Pevensey (Sussex) and no jugs are depicted. The table is set with trenchers and bowls and one diner is drinking from a bowl. In the Anglo-Norman period jugs were probably used to carry and serve liquids, such as wine for drinking and water for hand-washing. It is most likely that the bowls in use for drinking were made in wood rather than pottery, especially as the only known ceramic examples for this period are coarseware types. Although table 1 (*34*) shows that jugs comprise a relatively small percentage of the pottery from this period, they are notably more common than they were before the Conquest. In late Saxon Southampton no jugs were used at all. The equivalent vessel is a spouted pitcher, which could have been used for serving liquids, but is commonly identified as most suitable for storage. Thus, one of the most pronounced ceramic changes following the Norman Conquest was the adoption of the jug into the English pottery-makers' repertoire, and this must represent a shift in the use of pottery, perhaps stimulated by changes in dining habits.

THE HIGH MEDIEVAL PERIOD

The changes represented by the introduction of the jug into Anglo-Norman England seem to have become universal by about 1250. Figure *36* shows that, for the high medieval group from the Southampton assemblage, jugs comprise 47 per cent of the sherd weight while jars comprise 39 per cent by weight. This is remarkably different from the pattern observed for the Anglo-Norman period. The high medieval period is also characterised by an increased range of ceramic vessel types, including dripping pans and fire-covers (which are classified as 'Other' in figure *36*). The typical jar form (*colour plate 8* (1)) is related to the Anglo-Norman types and these vessels were probably still used mainly in the kitchen, either for storage or cooking. The variety of jug types is greatly increased and ranges from plain, unglazed, or partially glazed examples (*colour plate 8* (6,7)), which might have been used behind the scenes, to highly decorated forms that are commonly identified as tableware (*colour plate 8* (4)). At this period a great deal of pottery was imported from the Saintonge area of France, just north of Bordeaux, and this fine white ware is quite unlike anything produced locally and includes painted jugs that, to our eyes at least, are distinctly exotic in appearance (*colour plate 8* (8)).

It is clear that jugs served a variety of purposes, as containers of liquids in and around the kitchen and scullery, as chamber pots or bedpans, perhaps as cooking

	Rim Percent	Weight (g)	Sherd Count
Jar / Cooking pot	4531	73542	5160
Jug	4926	88998	5429
Pitcher	385	8668	305
Bowl	349	2094	109
Mortar	115	4796	33
Other	383	9029	230
Unidentified	671	47855	6013
Totals	11360	234982	17279

37 Table 2. Quantities of vessel types in the high medieval period from nine sites in Southampton

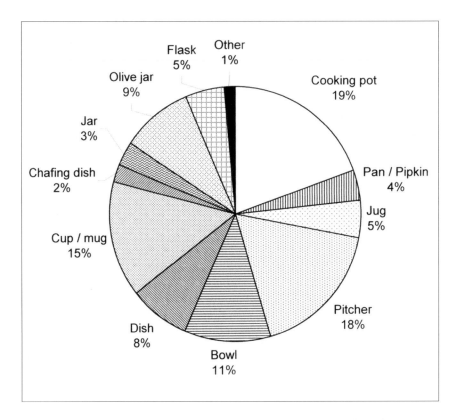

38 Pie chart representing the relative quantities by weight of late medieval vessel types shown in Table 3

	Rim percent	Weight (g)	Sherd count
Cooking pot	3158	29649	824
Pan / Pipkin	486	5714	119
Jug	755	7209	271
Pitcher	1299	26845	572
Bowl	762	17128	342
Dish	1503	11643	369
Cup / mug	2896	22256	986
Chafing dish	174	3501	64
Jar	337	4848	208
Olive jar	303	13664	458
Flask	830	7829	601
Other	192	2074	62
Unidentified	890	56315	4379
Totals	13585	208675	9255

39 Table 3. Quantities of vessel types in the late medieval period from nine sites in Southampton

vessels, but principally for the serving of wine and water at table. Other vessels that could also have been used at table include pégaux, three-handled pitchers made in the Saintonge district of southwestern France. These account for 4 per cent of the weight of high medieval pottery at Southampton. Pégaux are too large to have been really practicable for carrying liquids, however, and it seems more likely that they were used for mixing or storing wines; although some of them are highly decorated, and may have had a place at table. Pottery mortars were also imported from the Saintonge, although these are relatively scarce, at under 3 per cent of the high medieval group by weight. Those that do occur are often highly decorated with painted lines and applied human faces (*colour plate 9 (3)*) and as the presence of decoration is usually taken as an indicator that vessels were intended for display, mortars may perhaps have been used in tableside ceremonies such as the grinding of spices for wine. Bowls were also made in both coarseware and glazed sandy wares, but this is a rare ceramic form and most bowls were probably made from wood. Both wooden and ceramic bowls may also have been used at table, probably for drinking.

THE LATE MEDIEVAL PERIOD

Most of the late medieval pottery in Southampton derives from groups dated to the last decade of the fifteenth century, or the first decade of the sixteenth. Figure *38* shows that this period is characterised by a significant increase in the range of ceramic forms in use, and there is a corresponding increase in the range of sources represented. The local wares of this period are utilitarian in aspect, with virtually no decoration and minimal use of glaze, and take the form of plain jugs and jars (*40* (1)) and new types such as bunghole pitchers (*40* (3)) and large mixing bowls or pancheons (*40* (2)). Highly decorated tablewares were all brought into the town from distant sources: including cups and mugs from Surrey (*colour plate 9* (8)); stoneware mugs from the Rhineland, especially the Raeren area (*colour plate 9* (5)); brightly glazed or fine sgraffito-decorated mugs and dishes from Beauvais in northern France (*colour plate 9* (4)); painted dishes and brightly glazed chafing dishes (or plate-warmers: they had a crenellated rim upon which a dish would be placed and its contents kept warm by lighted charcoal in the bowl of the chafing dish) from the Saintonge (*colour plate 9* (7)); lustre-ware and tinglazed bowls and dishes from southern Spain (*colour plate 9* (9)); maiolica jugs, bowls and dishes from Italy, especially Tuscany (*colour plate 9* (2, 3)). All these types

Opposite: 40 Late medieval local pottery. 1: Late medieval well-fired sandy ware jar/cooking pot; 2: late medieval well-fired sandy ware pancheon; 3: Southampton organic-tempered sandy ware bunghole pitcher

occur together on a number of sites in large dumps of material backfilling stone structures such as garderobes and cellars, in association with substantial groups of Venetian glass. This sort of evidence suggests increasing sophistication at this period, as reflected in a significant demand for decorative tableware, which in turn may indicate a corresponding increase in the sophistication of mealtime ceremony and etiquette.

MEALTIME CEREMONY

Our understanding of the customary sequence of activities followed for each meal in the post-Conquest period has been gleaned from a variety of contemporary sources and may be summarised as follows. Once all diners were seated, the trenchers were cut, the salt cellar laid on the table and salt spooned onto each trencher. Hands were then washed with water brought in a jug. After grace the meat was carved at a side table or buffet and carried to the guests, who ate in messes – group of diners who shared food from the same dish. There were customs governing the numbers of diners of each rank that comprised a mess; higher nobility and clerics ate in messes of two, lesser nobility in threes and others in fours. Similar rules applied to how many dishes were served to each group; Edward III (1327-77) expected to receive eight dishes, his lords five, gentlemen three and grooms and others two. Edward IV (1461-70, 1471-83) commanded that in a mess, two men would share one loaf, four men a gallon of ale and three men one dish of meat or fish. Servants brought food to the table, ensured trenchers were clean or replaced if wet, and kept the table tidy and free from waste. They also had to refill any cups with ale or wine as soon as they became empty. Wine was often watered down, and when served with fruit or puddings, sweetened or spiced. These customs were applied at the highest levels of medieval society, and must therefore have been emulated by those lower down who had aspirations of gentility.

It is possible to identify pottery vessels with some of these activities, most notably the provision of water for washing, and the serving of wine. This latter activity was managed from the buffet, a sideboard where pitchers were kept for replenishing the cups of diners. At the higher echelons of society wine pitchers may more commonly have been made of precious metals, and thus the buffet became a vehicle for hosts to show off the best of their possessions, but it is possible to envisage the burgesses of a town such as Southampton utilising fine imported and locally-made earthenware as containers for wine at the buffet, and perhaps also incorporating some of them in the overall display. There were conventions, also, that governed the sorts of materials suited to different social classes, so that servants would not have been offered food or drink in precious metal vessels. It may be, therefore, that some of the pottery we associate with mealtime use was meant for use by more lowly diners, for many medieval meals included persons of varying rank.

In the Anglo-Norman and high medieval periods it is possible to understand ceramic tableware to be associated almost entirely with drinking. Although jugs may have been used in the washing of hands, they were obviously not designed for bringing food to the table, or for collecting scraps. Large pitchers, especially Saintonge pégaux, were perhaps more suited to the mixing or spicing of wine but standard sized jugs were most probably wielded by servants, or even drunk from directly. Pottery of the late medieval period includes a much wider variety of forms and a wide range of dining functions is suggested. There were still jugs for serving, but there were also cups and mugs for drinking from, while the wide variety of dishes and bowls may have been used for serving food, or perhaps as finger-bowls, and there were also chafing dishes for keeping food warm.

The importance of pottery as tableware seems to have grown throughout the later medieval period, and at the same time it is tempting to see this as evidence of an increase in the sophistication of dining custom, at least among the pottery-using classes. At the upper levels of medieval society, pottery may never have been considered worthy of use at table, at least not in comparison with metal and glass, but in the merchant households of a port such as Southampton, ceramics may have held greater significance. It is worth noting also that in the late medieval period pottery was imported into Southampton from a much wider range of sources, including Spain and Italy, and on a scale never matched before or since. This pottery was accompanied by a variety of exotic foodstuffs that perhaps also represent a change in eating habits, and thus mealtime custom.

SOCIAL DISTINCTIONS

The Southampton assemblage represents, more or less, pottery from households of equal social standing; merchants and burgesses of some wealth and influence, where playing host and displaying sophistication and largesse were important. It is therefore perhaps worth making a comparison with other types of dwelling in search of some understanding of where pottery might generally fit into the running of a household. The author has analysed pottery from a range of different settlements, including Bull Hall, a large town house in the port of Southampton, the house of wealthy merchant and sometime mayor, John de Tytynge, in the inland town of Winchester (Hants), Launceston Castle in Cornwall, a moated manor at Spencer's Farm in Berkshire and the rural farmstead of Wroughton

Copse in Wiltshire. A previous analysis of three of these assemblages has already been published (Brown, 1997) but there are now two new sites, Launceston and Spencer's Farm, to add to the exercise. All these assemblages are broadly contemporary, dating to the last part of the thirteenth century.

Figure *41* presents a pie chart for each site that shows the range of vessel types used in each dwelling. Jugs and related tableware comprise over 50 per cent of the assemblages at the town houses in Southampton and Winchester, and this may reflect a high level of consumption of liquids, especially in a mealtime context. At Launceston Castle, jars and jugs are present in equal quantities, but here, at the home of the Earls of Cornwall, there may have been high quantities of metal vessels in use and on display. A castle can be viewed as a place that played host to a wider variety of people of all classes, including soldiers, servants and labourers, than the town houses of merchants. Launceston may also be characterised as a place of work, where a variety of activities, including the processing of foods, was carried out, on a much larger scale than in an urban setting. This would also have been true at Spencer's Farm, which was undoubtedly lower down the social scale than Launceston Castle and was probably part farm and part manor. This is reflected in the high number of bowls of wide, shallow form that were probably used in processing milk. There are also large numbers of these at Wroughton Copse, where, unsurprisingly, glazed jugs are few. This place is truly within the lowest levels of medieval society, where there would have been no entertaining and no pretensions towards the sorts of behaviour recommended in treatises on etiquette.

This exercise has shown that pottery occurs in different quantities at different types of site, and can help to provide some understanding of its relative value to different sectors of society. In an urban context pottery was easily obtained and seems to have been consumed at a relatively high rate. Here, jugs were very important and this suggests that they were utilised more frequently at mealtimes, whereas in a castle this may not have been so much the case, and in any case it is likely that the lord may not have valued pottery very highly. In truly rural contexts, also, it is not possible to place pottery in a dining context. This therefore shows how, although the ceramic record in Southampton demonstrates the increasing complexity, versatility and therefore worth to the consumer of pottery throughout the medieval period, this view has to be balanced by an understanding of context.

CONCLUSION

While this is not a particularly complex analysis of the ceramic evidence for medieval mealtime custom, if any one conclusion might be drawn it would be that if we were to base our understanding of medieval manners entirely on the archaeological evidence, then we would have little appreciation of the value placed on courtly behaviour and gentility. This may, of course, mean that despite the historical sources, medieval people really did have no manners and dwelt continuously in a brutish fug of oafishness and ignorance, but actually the refinement and charm of so many medieval artefacts found during excavation, serves to refute any such claim. What is clear, therefore, is that the archaeological evidence is deficient.

This is brought home on those rare occasions when an excavation produces a wide range of artefacts made of those perishable materials that rarely survive in the ground. A good example of this is the late thirteenth-century fill of a stone-lined pit excavated by Colin Platt at Cuckoo Lane, Southampton (Platt and Coleman-Smith 1975). Waterlogged conditions enabled the survival of a wide range of material types, including wood, leather, textile, rope and basketry. The publication of this group shows that 46 pots were recovered, while there were remains of 71 wooden objects, including a dozen turned bowls. Very few of the pottery vessels were bowls, and this example highlights the relationship between different materials, and emphasizes the need for archaeologists to remain aware of this. Most of those bowls were probably used for drinking

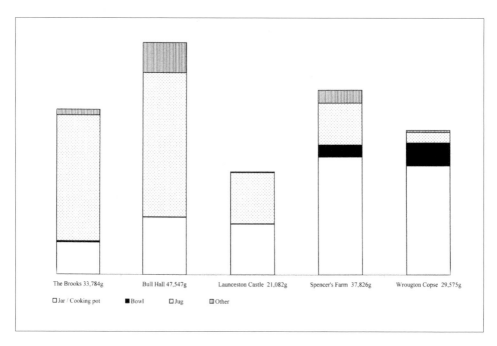

41 Bar chart showing the relative quantities of jar/cooking pots, jugs, bowls and other vessels in late thirteenth-century phases at five different dwellings

from or serving food, both functions that are scarcely reflected in the pottery assemblage. The one complements the other. This is brought home also in the late medieval groups, where glass and pottery was deposited in large quantities. This shows that although pottery was becoming more sophisticated and indeed suited to a wider variety of purposes, the urban consumer was prepared to invest in more expensive, exotic materials as a means of displaying taste, refinement and sophistication.

It is still the case, notwithstanding, that such aspects of the human condition remain elusive to archaeological analysis, for there is little direct, material, evidence for the development of mealtime etiquette. It is hoped that this study has shown how material culture can be understood to reflect custom and social practice, and thus provide a link between what is written and what can be found, even if it may rarely provide evidence for specific actions. If this has helped to identify areas for future research then so much the better.

Duncan Brown

ACKNOWLEDGEMENTS

References to documentary sources are derived from Hammond (1993) and Scully (1995).

BIBLIOGRAPHY

Brown, D.H., 'Pottery and late Saxon Southampton', *Proceedings of the Hampshire Field Club Archaeological Society*, 50 (1995), pp.127–52
— , 'Pots from houses', *Medieval Ceramics*, 21 (1997), pp.83–94
— , *Pottery in Medieval Southampton c.1066-1510*, Southampton Archaeology Monographs 8, Council for British Archaeology Research Report 133 (London, 2002)
Hammond, P.W., *Food and Feast in Medieval England* (Stroud, 1993)
Platt, C. and Coleman-Smith, R., *Excavations in Medieval Southampton, 1953-1969*, 2 vols (Leicester, 1975)
Scully, T., *The Art of Cookery in the Middle Ages* (Woodbridge, 1995)

seven

DINING IN DISHARMONY
IN THE LATER MIDDLE AGES

Many studies have explored the ways in which medieval elite dining practices brought together people of diverse social rank and reinforced the social order through such means as seating arrangements, table settings, the processes of serving food, the rituals surrounding dining, the food consumed and so on. Recent accounts have observed that the act of eating in public was an event during which the lord and the guest demonstrated their respective status, and as Elaine Clark has commented 'the stately banquets of princes and nobles … represented exclusive affairs designed and elaborately staged to enhance bonds of privilege and rank'. Dining at a lord's residence also reinforced the sense of mutual dependency of the lord and their visitors, many of whom were servants and employees.

Yet, when exploring the evidence for later medieval dining among the lay aristocracy of England and France one is struck by the evidence for disastrous and disharmonious dining occasions. Documentary sources elucidate meals punctuated by illness, murder, fighting, illicit sexual unions and broken tableware. Meanwhile the material culture of dining includes items of tableware and furnishings from dining spaces likely to have caused social embarrassment or unease. In this chapter I shall suggest that, although dining was certainly an important and regular occasion for reinforcing social ties, at the same time it was a risky enterprise laden with opportunity for disharmony, sometimes exacerbated by the very locations and material culture of dining. This chapter draws heavily on documentary sources, and in doing so seeks to throw new light on the idealised images of feasts by medieval artists and to place items of dining-related material culture that are commonly treated as mere frippery or decoration into a broader and somewhat different social context.

DINING IN HARMONY

I shall begin by briefly examining contemporary views of how aristocratic dining was supposed to be conducted. The dining practices of the later medieval aristocracy of England and France appear to have been highly formalised affairs, according to both documentary evidence – including conduct books and chronicles – and manuscript illuminations of dining scenes. Such sources suggest that dining consisted of a series of stages and that the dining experience within aristocratic households varied according to a person's status. The meal was preceded by the setting up of the dining room and the laying of the tables, the summons to table, and a process of formalised hand-washing (*colour plate 10*). Diners were then seated according to rank, with the lord, his immediate family and honoured guests on the main table usually located at the dais end of the hall, with other diners sat at tables commonly arranged at right angles to that of the lord. Diners at the lord's table would normally be served first, and would probably be provided with the finest tableware, their own dishes, drinking vessels, spoons and knives, whereas diners at other tables would wait to be served, would share dishes and cups and may have to provide their own knives, spoons and cups.

The behaviour of diners, especially lower ranking members of the household, was prescribed in conduct books and manuals of household management. They were exhorted not to lean on the table, or dirty the cloth, nor to talk with a full mouth, break wind or look at what comes out of their nose when blown. The importance of sharing at the table was stressed. Lords, meanwhile, were advised to be hospitable and generous, but to keep their household in good order and avoid waste. For example, in the 1240s Bishop Grosseteste of Lincoln advised the Countess of Lincoln to attend meals in the great hall and courteously distributing food 'that your presence … is made manifest to all', but at the same time as exercising largesse there should be good order in the household and avoidance of waste. As Christopher Dyer has observed, 'the object seemed to be to present a superficial sociability to the outside world, while behind the scenes a constant coercion kept underlings in control'.

Menus could often be very elaborate, with many courses, particularly on special feast days, of which there were many in the later medieval period. Dining, especially when important guests were present, was often accompanied by some form of entertainment. This included musicians, tumblers, mummers, storytellers and so-called entremets or sotelties, which were impressive table decorations, including elaborately decorated boars' heads, peacocks and swans (*42, 43*).

42 Servants and musicians attend the royal table. Redrawn from the Queen Mary Psalter of the early fourteenth century

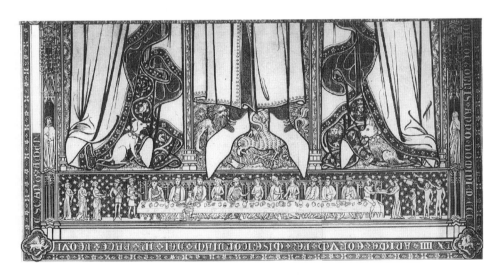

43 Peacock feast. Detail of the presentation of a peacock at a feast, from the monumental brass of Robert Braunche (d. 1364) at St Margaret's Church in King's Lynn (Norfolk). Musicians and servants are also depicted

EXAMPLES OF DISASTROUS DINING

There have been many publications expanding on these elaborate dining rituals. However, these were ideals and the content and proliferation of conduct books suggests that there was a contemporary recognition that behaviour might not always be so measured. Moreover, and more generally, recent research on both the later medieval Church and the aristocratic household reveals that dining occupied a socially and morally ambivalent position. Food featured in the celebration of the Eucharist, which emphasised its positive connotations, but the sin of gluttony was the result of the abuse of food, and was a common enough motif in the borders of medieval illuminated manuscripts (*44*): Elizabeth Biebel has described gluttony as 'a dark parallel of the Eucharist'. Meanwhile, the great households had to balance the social requirements of lordly largesse with hard economics and the need to live within their means. Contemporary commentary criticised excessive displays of food designed more to please the eye than to fill the stomach, and ridiculed and condemned lords who ate well at the expense of others while providing meagre offerings at their own table. The hapless Henry III of England (1216-72) brought shame on himself with the poor quality of his Christmas feast in 1250 and in subsequent years by appearing to spend more time eating in the houses of others than distributing largesse in his own halls.

Aside from having to negotiate the intricacies of ecclesiastical teachings and contemporary social demands, the aristocratic dinner was sometimes too elaborate to be successfully completed. At a dinner given by Charles VI of France (1380-1422) in honour of Queen Isabella of France (1385-1422) in 1389 in Paris, the hall was very crowded and after the guests had washed their hands and sat down things got out of hand:

> some were made ill by the heat, or fainted in the crowd. A table near the door of the parliament chamber was overturned by force. The ladies who were sitting at it had to get up hurriedly, without ceremony. The great heat and the stink of the crowd almost caused the Queen to faint, and the window which was behind her had to be broken to let in the air … The King saw what was happening and ordered the performance to stop. This was done and the tables were quickly cleared and taken down to give the ladies more room. The wine and spices were served hurriedly and, as soon as the King and Queen had gone to their apartments, everyone else left also.

The implications of this turn of events do not appear to have been serious, perhaps because the feast was only one of a series of events to mark the entry of the new queen into Paris, but it reveals the difficulties of maintaining order among large numbers of excitable diners. At another of Charles VI's banquets,

44 Gluttony. This image from the fourteenth-century Luttrell Psalter (fo. 157v) has been interpreted variously as a medieval party-trick or as a form of water-torture. More recently Michael Camille has suggested that the image of a man being glutted with wine represents the sin of gluttony. He suggests that this interpretation is reinforced by the knife sticking out of his pocket; in a contemporary English devotional lyric Christ contrasts the fashionable dress of courtiers, with a wide split and knife sticking out to the side, with his own suffering body during the Passion

entertainers dressed as wild men were burned alive. Sometimes the formalities of dining created logistical problems. For example, instructions in a fifteenth-century conduct book on how to carve a crab at the dining table reveal a ritual so complex that it is built into the procedure that the food has to be returned to the kitchen to be reheated: such rituals, and the great distance of kitchens from the hall in many castles and manor houses meant that complaints about cold food are not uncommon in medieval accounts of dining.

On other occasions the provision of food and drink as a harmonious social act was prone to subversion by the opportunity provided by large social gatherings for misdemeanours of various sorts. The dining hall provided a good location for political intrigue. A row between two of his earls caused Richard II of England (1377-99) to abandon one dinner in 1389; and this was a meal that had, in fact, been encouraged on him by the Earl Marshall trying to engineer a situation in which he could expose the supposed treachery of the Earl of Derby.

At a feast held by Richard shortly afterwards hardly any of the nobility turned up, so hostile were they to the king. Indeed, the latter part of Richard's reign is peppered with feasts that few would attend. They were wise to avoid them, as Richard's troublesome uncle, the Duke of Gloucester, was to discover when washing his hands ready for dinner in the castle at Calais (France), where he was, according to some accounts, strangled with the towel by his enemies. The political significance of dining is demonstrated elsewhere during Richard II's reign, when in the course of the campaign in Ireland 1394-5, one of his leading lords, Henry Chrystede, was appointed to negotiate with four Irish kings who had come to Dublin to submit to the English king. Chrystede disapproved of the manner of dining of these kings, which included such intolerable practices as permitting servants and minstrels to dine alongside them, and on the fourth day of his interaction with them Chrystede rearranged the dining room in what, to him at least, was a more appropriate fashion. The Irish kings at first refused to eat in such a manner, but were eventually convinced that dining in the 'correct' manner was a necessary element of political submission.

Fines imposed on servants for not performing their duties properly and for theft indicate that those who role it was to implement the exercise of lordly largesse might sometimes fail to do so appropriately. Meanwhile, legislation to prevent mumming by strangers indicates fear that they would use the opportunity of disguise to commit crime. The incorporation of English minstrels into a gild in 1469 was a response to tales of 'rough peasants and craftsmen' receiving great sums of money by pretending to be minstrels. Fear of poisoning was also often acutely felt. In 1388 the Count de Foix was warned that his son – who normally served his dishes and tasted his food – intended to poison him. The count snatched the poison from his son at the table, and fed it to his greyhound, which dropped dead – thus exposing the son's treachery. In 1391 the count did not, however, even get as far as the table, collapsing as water was poured over his hands by attendants, who promptly drank the water in order to demonstrate that they had not poisoned it. The fear of potential poisoning was reflected in the staged testing of food by servants prior to serving, and by the demand for tableware made of materials believed to reveal the presence of poison, such as unicorn horn.

Didactic literature often refers to the potential social dangers of various dining scenarios. In a conduct manual written by the Knight of the Tour Landry for his daughters in the late fourteenth century, he advises them on good behaviour through a series of exempla. A number involve dining. For example, the knight warns his daughters not to attend feasts alone – not so much because they might have evil befall them, but because of the evil things others might *say* about them. He recalls a lady who was seen talking alone to a knight at a feast, explaining that this was sufficient cause for there never again to be peace between the woman and her husband. He also tells the story of two young women hurrying to a feast to show off their new clothes. They took a shortcut over a morass and fell in, and were subsequently mocked at the feast for their vanity. Another woman who refused to eat with her husband was punished when he set up a table in the kitchen and invited the swineherd to join his wife for dinner. The wife wept at being served in this humiliating manner. This text highlights the social risks taken by women who visit other households unaccompanied, and the importance of maintaining a public show of unity with their husbands while dining. Conduct books hint at the social power of gossip, an aspect of them that has received far less attention from scholars than the advice about table manners. If reputations could be made at dinner in the great households of the later Middle Ages, then they could also be ruined by malicious gossip about the events, real or imagined, that occurred on such occasions.

DINING AND THE UNEXPECTED

Inversions of the normal hierarchy of dining could be used to great political or pious effect. Following the capture of King John II of France (1350-64) in 1356, Edward, the Black Prince of England (1330-76) insisted on serving the king at dinner – and although it is difficult to read the motives of the prince, whether he was attempting to rub salt into the king's wounds or humbling himself before the king in order to facilitate negotiations, his actions were sufficiently unusual to prompt contemporary comment. The chronicler Jean Froissart remarked that the esteem of both the English and the French for the prince increased as a result of this act. When King Louis IX of France (1226-70) washed the feet of beggars in the early thirteenth century his chronicler, Joinville, expressed horror at this event – but Louis was able to invoke biblical sanction for his action, in the form of Jesus washing the feet of his disciples at the Last Supper. Nonetheless, the contemporary unease with such ritualised inversions may, as Bridget Ann Henisch has suggested, be reflected in the medieval formation of the legend of St Martial, who was said to have helped Jesus at the Last Supper by performing the menial tasks of carrying water and towels. Humility by the great had its political and pious uses, but it was rarely uncomplicated and had to be carefully staged.

Within medieval literature, the feast is an occasion at which the magnificence of the lord is demonstrated, but is also frequently a moment when the unexpected occurs. In the medieval Arthurian tradition, Arthur often delays eating until he has been enthralled by some strange and marvellous tale of knightly deeds, or until some stranger has entered the hall and sought leave to challenge one of the Round Table, such as the Green Knight who was to set a challenge for Sir Gawain. Literary feasts also afforded opportunities to humiliate a host. At the feast to celebrate his coronation Arthur was snubbed by the Scottish kings who refused to accept gifts from 'a beardless boy of low birth'. In another Arthurian tale, the entry of Sir Degrevant into the hall of a neighbouring earl as the household was eating reinforced the public shame of the earl who had recently broken a promise.

In the fourteenth-century tale of Sir Orfeo the hero uses disguise as a minstrel to gain entry to a dining hall, first to retrieve his wife, and, later, to reassert lordship in his own castle. Although the latter event brought the tale to a happy conclusion, the dining room was commonly the location for social stress within medieval literature, as guests either did not know, or chose to ignore, the proper social conventions surrounding the receipt of hospitality. Concern about the behaviour of guests is reflected in conduct books, which largely regulate the behaviour of guests, sometimes by agonising over situations that are unlikely ever to have arisen, such as what to do with the assertive parents of the pope trying to claim equality of status with their son. In doing so, such texts were reflecting the vulnerability of good order in the household to the assertiveness of strangers who might not know their place. As Felicity Heal has recently observed of the symbolic world of the great households of the later Middle Ages, 'its capacity to enforce the specific conception of its head was uncertain, and the possibilities of subversion were ever present', especially in the face of guests whose behaviour might be unpredictable.

THE MATERIAL CULTURE OF MEDIEVAL DINING

The material culture of high-status dining spaces, both tableware and items decorating the hall or chamber, sometimes appears to have had the potential to frustrate or humiliate. These include items such as puzzle jugs, in which liquid was held in two separate chambers, and which would flood the unwary drinker with liquid – the trick being to negotiate the system of mouth pieces, hollow handles and rims (45) – while a striking jug found at Exeter (Devon) holds liquid despite appearing to be incapable of doing so (46). A fourteenth-century maplewood mazer from Corpus Christ College, Cambridge with silver-gilt has a hollow central column topped by battlements within which is a swan which will tip liquid over the unwary drinker if the bowl is filled above the level of the battlements. The thirteenth-century French architect Villard de Honnecourt described how to make a similar cup using hollow devices and tubes in which the drinker's lips never manage to reach the wine, while a little bird perched at the brim appears to drink away contentedly:

45 Puzzle jug from Oxford. This jug has two chambers, of which the lower one is filled through the hollow handle at the side and liquid flows out through the stag's-head spout. The drinker would be tempted to drink from the opposite side to the stag's-head spout, and would be soaked by liquid held in the upper chamber, which would pour out through the second spout

Here is a siphon which may be made in a cup in such a way that there is a little tower in its middle, and in the middle of that a tube reaching down to the bottom of the cup. The tube must be as long as the cup is deep. And in the tower there must be three cross-channels against the bottom of the cup so that the wine in the cup may go into the tube. Above the tower, there should be a bird with its beak held so low that it may drink when the cup is full. The wine will then flow through the tube and the foot of the cup, which is double. The bird should obviously be hollow too.

Most authors simply pass over such items as examples of the medieval sense of humour, but they take on a different guise when seen in the context of the humiliation of guests outlined in the exampla from didactic literature – such as the tale from the book of the Knight of the Tour-Landry of a knight who pretended to mistake another knight for a minstrel in order to teach him a lesson about the unusual coat he was wearing.

46 Puzzle jug from
Saintonge (France). A
late thirteenth-century
polychrome ware jug
found at Exeter (Devon).
Liquid poured into
the mouth of the jug
passes down through the
hollow handle, across the
base and out through
the spout, although the
open spaces of the jug,
designed to look like
a building, conveys the
impression that it cannot
possibly hold any liquid

The number of perplexing drinking vessels is not great, and it is difficult to judge whether they really would have tricked drinkers into a soaking or whether, on the contrary, their function would have been well-known, and the drinker would have been tempted to risk a soaking in order to prove their skill at the challenge. It may be relevant to note that the words of medieval songs hint at forfeits to be paid if diners did not join in the entertainment on offer, with a ditty or a dance, and it may be that such trick drinking vessels presented a similar social pressure.

Table decorations are also generally regarded as mere fun, yet the potential to use them to make serious points was not missed. For example, the sotelties at the coronation banquet for Henry V of England (1413-22) in 1413 included a swan holding a message asking 'have pity on the realm', presumably an embodiment of political hope. Sixteen years later the sotelties for the coronation feast of his successor, Henry VI (1437-61), had more controversial aims, stressing the unity of the French and English nations under one, English, king. They included a depiction of The Virgin with child holding out the crown of England to Henry, while St Denis of France and St George of England looked on approvingly. Attached to this was the message that Henry was born by descent and by right 'Justly to reigne in England and in France'. However, this claim ignored the coronation of Charles VII as king of France four months earlier, and at just eight years of age Henry VI was hardly in a position to challenge the French king. A late fifteenth-century English manuscript outlining the appropriate arrangements for a wedding feast recommends a sotelty depicting the wife lying in child-bed. A harmless enough ambition, perhaps, but one that reminded the newly married couple of their dynastic responsibilities. The implications of these accounts of sotelties is that they were not designed by the host but by whoever was responsible for organising the meal, and the intentions of the two parties may have differed. At a dinner given in 1378 by King Charles VI of France for the emperor of Bohemia and his son the sotelty was a dramatic reconstruction with actors of the capture of Jerusalem by the crusaders nearly two centuries earlier – it has been suggested that this was arranged by one of the king's counsellors who had been lobbying for years to persuade various European rulers to embark on another crusade.

It is possible to interpret trick drinking vessels, sotelties, plays and other performances while dining as a safety-valve for elite society, providing an opportunity for the lower orders to let off steam, sometimes through a temporary inversion of the social order. However, it did not always work, sometimes tipping over into real disorder, or proving too offensive for the lord to accept. This, at least, appears to have been the fate of John Atte Forth of Polstead (Suff) who in 1363 was fined for having played 'a summer game' in the lord's hall, with which the lord was not amused.

The setting in which the aristocratic household dined also possessed the potential to subvert the possibility of harmonious dining. Henry III of England had three of his great halls (at Ludgershall (Wilts), (Northants) and Guildford (Surrey)) painted with the story of Dives, the rich man tortured with thirst in Hell because he had ignored the beggar Lazarus at his gates. Henry's wall paintings would have served as reminders of the importance of helping the needy. But almsgiving was an awkward social event – few lords were prepared to invite the poor into their halls more than once a year, and for the rest of the time preferred to feed them at their gates, or to see them deposited in the almshouses they subsidised. The reciprocal prayers of the poor were handy for ensuring eternal salvation, but this seemingly did not compensate for the distasteful fact of their daily presence. Moreover, although reminders of the perils of failure to be suitably charitable were acceptable within churches, the elite do not normally seem to have used such motifs in the context of domestic dining. In the case of Henry III wall-paintings emphasising the dangers of a lack of charity may have sat uneasily alongside his reputation as a miserly host (see above).

Decoration on tapestries and wall-paintings and on the more elaborate tableware more commonly espoused the chivalric ethos of later medieval society. Examples include jugs decorated with knights on horseback, such as those produced in the kilns at Scarborough (Yorks) (49). Mazers and bowls sometimes depicted scenes of knightly prowess. Examples include a late fourteenth-century mazer with a medallion depicting the legendary Guy of Warwick showing the earl on horseback and inscribed 'Guy of Warwick is his name: here he kills the dragon', and what is probably a spice dish of the early fourteenth century, depicting a knight kneeling at the feet of his lady. Metal and ceramic aquamaniles in the shape of riders on horseback are also known, including a late thirteenth-century copper-alloy example found in the River Tyne (47). The hall might be decorated with tapestries depicting battles, such as that on the famous feast scene from the Duke de Berry's early fifteenth-century book of hours (*colour plate 10*), scenes from ancient epic and heroic battles, or hunt scenes, such as those on the famous fifteenth-century tapestries from Hardwick Hall (Derbys). The messages of tapestries and wall-paintings were sometimes enhanced by the inclusion of written commentaries among the imagery and by the occasional presence of a story-teller whose role it was to elucidate this artwork to guests. This suggests that such decorations were often carefully chosen to convey specific messages or ideas, and the same may be true of tableware as well. Indeed, two English late fourteenth-century metal jugs carry mottoes of advice for diners. One warns:

> He that wyl not spare when he may (He that shall not save as he can)
> He shal not spend when he would (Shall not spend when he wants to)
> Deme the best in every dowt (Suppose the best in every fear)
> Til the trowthe be tryid (Until the truth is known)

while the other jug is inscribed:

> + Goddis Grace be in this place Amen + (God's grace be in this place, amen')
> Stond utter from the fyre (stand away from the fire)
> And lat on iust come nere (and let just one come near)

Some tableware was not used very often, but was rather displayed in the hall on a dresser (or cup board) for diners to view, presumably serving to impress

47 A late thirteenth-century copper-alloy aquamanile. The lance, shield, lid of helmet, the knight's feet and the horse's tail are missing. The aquamanile would have been filled through the top of the helmet and poured through the spout on the forehead of the horse

them with the wealth and connections of the host: the cup board was the star attraction in the hall during the aforementioned feast for Queen Isabella. Indeed, guidelines on stacking the cup board are often included in conduct books. Yet, if the material culture of the dining room had messages to convey, then one assumes that there might also be room for debate, in particular about the appropriateness of the associations of the imagery with the host. One wonders what would have been the implications of martial display following military defeat, at times of political unrest, if the lord had never fought, or was now too old to do so, or when guests included churchmen who did not always approve of the nature of secular culture.

48 A fourteenth-century face jug. This example was found in London, from where a considerable number of jugs in human form have been recovered

Decorative items from the dining room were not merely reflections of lordly aspirations, but they were of themselves part of the performance of lordship. This lordship was also overwhelmingly masculine, and the great households were largely comprised of men. Given this, we may wonder about the reception of such displays of knightly prowess when the male head of a household was away, or when the head of a household was a woman, a common enough occurrence in the fourteenth and fifteenth centuries, delaying many men from attaining their full inheritance. In this context apparently 'fun' items such as face jugs take on a different guise. They largely depict male faces, often with beards (*48*), which in medieval thought represented mature masculinity and virility, while beardless

49 A late thirteenth-century knight jug. This jug from Scarborough has knights on horseback around the rim facing towards the spout, which is in the form of a man

men were regarded with suspicion, and occasionally venom, and were perceived as feminine. Although such jugs are found across a range of sites, within the elite dining hall – packed with men – they were used in what was essentially a process of homosocial bonding, and must have played a part, however small, in reinforcing the masculine world of the medieval castle.

Other contentious aspects of the material culture of dining may be briefly highlighted. First, much tableware and many tapestries appear to have been acquired as booty during warfare – in the wake of victory to display such items may have been acceptable, but what about when the political tide turned? Second, while higher status guests were better provided for at table, this did mean that they had to sup from the tableware of their host, often laden with his insignia. Meanwhile the lower status guests were often required to bring their own tableware, providing them with an opportunity, albeit small-scale, to display their own affiliations and interests through decoration on their knives and drinking vessels. Indeed, the level of decoration on the handles and scabbards of knives suggests that they were prized possessions, while the evidence of wills suggests that cups were important personal items, often given pet names, and providing a focus for memories. Third, there are the complaints made by commentators such as William Langland and Robert Mannyng about lords withdrawing from the hall, and dining in their own chambers, which serve as reminders of the pressures guests and the wider household placed on lords. Finally, the conduct books to which I have referred, while ostensibly concerned with the regulation of elite dining practices, increasingly found a market among the urban and middling classes. They could not have hoped to dine in the ways prescribed, and thus the conduct books took on a new mantle as status symbols of the socially aspirant. It has also been suggested by Claire Sponsler that as food became relatively more plentiful in the wake of massive population decline from the late fourteenth century, the capacity of food consumption to 'create and disseminate cultural meanings' expanded, and advice about how to regulate the consumption of food would have become increasingly welcome by newly prosperous households.

DINING AND THE NON–DINER

Caroline Walker Bynum has drawn attention to instances of exceptionally pious medieval women whose abstention from eating and generous distribution of food to the poor turned mealtimes into a battleground. The *vitae* of female saints include numerous examples of women who did not eat normally – some like Douceline of Marseilles (d. 1274) and Jane Mary of Maillé (d. 1414) were nourished by the Eucharist and refused food at other times, while Beatrice of Ornacieux (d. 1310) was allegedly prevented from eating after a crumb from the Host remained in her mouth causing it to swell up. Margery Kempe (*c.* 1373-1438) of Kings Lynn (Norfolk), in the early fifteenth century experienced a dramatic spiritual crisis, and caused her husband great consternation with her abstinence from food, as well as her sexual continence. Her peculiar eating practices and her tendency to give away food from her buttery was eventually used by Margery as a bargaining tool: she agreed to return to normal social dining practices in return for not having to have sex with her husband. As Walker Bynum has observed, refusal to eat and voluntary fasting were effective means for individuals, especially women, to coerce and criticise their family and friends. Both the family and the household are social units that reside and above all eat together; thus, as Walker Bynum says, to refuse to partake of this commensality and to give away the contents of the family cupboard is 'to refuse the meal as symbol of the familial bond', and to reject the money and household management skills that produced the meal. Furthermore, although almsgiving was advocated by the Church, excessive food distribution might be perceived as a threat to the charitable role and hierarchy of the Church.

CONCLUSION

The stylised and orderly feasts in manuscript illuminations present dining as the elite wished it to be perceived, and they reflect the importance of prestigious display for the maintenance of social distinctions. Yet, as we have seen, things did not always work out as planned. Moreover, even the idealised illuminated scenes are not straightforward. The frequent use of the medieval feast scene from the fourteenth-century Luttrell Psalter as an illustration of the archetypal medieval dinner has recently been questioned (*colour plate 11*). Art historian Michael Camille has argued that this scene was, in fact, an expression of acute anxiety about the Luttrell family's spiritual and social status. When the manuscript was commissioned there was no heir in the second generation and Geoffrey Luttrell had recently sought papal sanction of his marriage of many years, having discovered that he and his wife were so closely related as to breach the Church's laws of consanguinity. Camille has argued that this meal was held at Epiphany, essentially a feast looking to the future, and has suggested that the feast scene has to be saved from being a sinful, gluttonous image by its pseudo-sacred ceremonial, mirroring the Last Supper image elsewhere in the manuscript.

50 A medieval fight. Two individuals, half man and half beast, fight, as one hits the other with a jug. *Redrawn from the Luttrell Psalter by Jess Earnshaw*

Recent work by archaeologists on the dwelling places of the aristocracy has explored the impact of moving through such buildings on guests, highlighting the disadvantages for disoriented visitor in an unfamiliar environment, under the watchful eyes of the lord's retainers, forced to submit to the social order of the lord in order to receive hospitality. While I do not disagree with that, the material I have discussed suggests that the lord and his household were potentially as threatened or disconcerted by the visitor. My purpose in this chapter has been to remind us of the need not to be seduced by the harmonious images of Merry England presented both in the pages of secondary literature and in many of the medieval depictions of dining. We should also remember that medieval dining was not simply a symbolic ritual, but was a practical component of the negotiation of medieval social and political relations, and as such we should not underestimate either the possibility for subversion of the elite's intentions, or the potentially transformative effect – sometimes for the worse – of dining on existing social relationships.

D.M. Hadley

ACKNOWLEDGEMENTS

I would like to thank Maureen Carroll, Oliver Jessop and Hugh Willmott for their comments on an earlier draft of this paper, and Duncan Brown, Paul Blinkhorn and Chris Cumberpatch for useful discussion of later medieval pottery. I am grateful to Jess Earnshaw and Oliver Jessop for preparing illustrations. The following institutions gave permission for the reproduction of images: The British Library (fig. *44* and *colour plate 11*), The British Museum (fig. *47*), The Ashmolean Museum (fig. *45*), Museum of London (fig. *48*), The Bibliothèque Nationale in Paris (*colour plate 10*), and Royal Albert Memorial Museum in Exeter (fig. *46*).

BIBLIOGRAPHY

Bynum, C.W., *Holy Feast and Holy Fast: the religious significance of food to medieval women* (Berkeley, 1987)
Carlin, M. and Roesenthal, J., *Food and Eating in Medieval Europe* (London, 1997)
Clark, E., 'Social welfare and mutual aid in the medieval countryside', *Journal of British Studies*, 33 (1994), pp.381-406

Furnivall, F.J. (ed.), *The Babees Book: manners and meals in olden times* (London, 1868)

Hammond, P.W., *Food and Feast in Medieval England* (Stroud, 1993)

Heal, F., 'Reciprocity and exchange in the late medieval household', in B. Hanawalt and D. Wallace (eds), *Bodies and Disciplines* (Minneapolis, 1996), pp.179-98

Henisch, B.A., *Fast and Feast: food in medieval society* (London, 1986)

Mead, W. *The English Medieval Feast* (London, 1931)

Scully, T., *The Art of Cookery in the Middle Ages* (Woodbridge, 1995)

Sponsler, C., 'Eating lessons: Lydgate's "Dietary" and consumer conduct', in K. Ashley and R. Clark (eds), *Medieval Conduct* (Minneapolis, 2001), pp.1-22

eight

TUDOR DINING:
OBJECT AND IMAGE AT THE TABLE

Dining was one of the most important social acts in Tudor cultural life. One sixteenth-century Venetian observed that the English thought 'no greater honour can be conferred, or received, than to invite others to eat with them or be invited themselves'. Therefore, it is not surprising that dining was a formalised and complex affair, and that it was within this arena that an increasing number of tablewares were used during the Tudor period.

This chapter has two aims. The first is concerned with outlining the nature of dining in Tudor England. The subject of late medieval and renaissance feasting has received significant historical attention. However, this work has primarily concentrated on the preparation, presentation and consumption of foodstuffs, and not the role that tablewares played at the table. Accordingly, this chapter will examine several eye-witness accounts of sixteenth-century dining and explore the arena in which objects were used. The second aim of this chapter is to investigate briefly some of the meanings held by dining culture, through the examination of a specific case study, that of engraved glass drinking vessels.

THE PROGRESS OF THE MEAL

William Harrison, writing in 1587, gives one of the most comprehensive insights into dining in England during the late Tudor period. One important point addressed by Harrison concerns both the number and timing of meals. He says that prior to the sixteenth century there were two meals a day. He further elaborates on the timing of these two meals by saying that:

the nobilitie, gentrie, and students doo ordinarilie go to dinner at eleven before noone, and to supper at five ... the merchants dine and sup seldome before twelve noone and six at night ... the husbandmen dine also at high noone as they call it and sup at seven or eight ... As for the poorest sort they generaillie dine and sup when they may.

Harrison's assertion that only two meals a day were eaten is probably misleading. Other written sources, such as the account book of Henry Percy Duke of Northumberland in 1512, show that breakfast, at least in a rich household, was quite varied, with dishes that included beef, mutton and fish. In mentioning just two regulated meals, Harrison seems to be emphasising his perception of greater control of his own time, as opposed to the gluttony and over-eating of the past. Whatever the case may be, it would appear that only dinner and supper were large-scale events. Harrison's timings of the meals were probably a more accurate reflection of reality, dinner being served around mid-day and supper early evening. This pattern would fit with the schedule formally observed in monastic institutions, where meals were taken after the services of Nones and Vespers.

When describing the course of the meal, Harrison does not give a complete description of one from start to finish. However, he does give certain insights into some of the practicalities and rituals that occurred. He emphasises the hierarchy that still existed at the table, similar to the medieval pattern, which involved:

the principall tables whereat the nobleman, his ladie and guestes are accustomed to side; beside which they have certain ordinarie allowance dailie appointed for their hals, where the chiefe officers and household servants ... and with them such inferior guestes doo feed

Harrison also makes further comments on the number of diners, the way people drank and the number of dishes used. All these lend an important insight into the process of dining.

DINING OF THE ELITE

In addition to Harrison there are several interesting eyewitness accounts of notable occasions in which the meal was described in close detail. Two of these were concerned with dinners served to Queen Elizabeth I. Both the people who observed these occasions were German travellers who were allowed to watch, but not participate. Lupold von Wedel saw the Queen dine at Greenwich on the 27 December 1584. Initially, a long table was set and covered, presumably with the knives, napkins and the salt. Then 40 gilt dishes were brought in and set before the Queen, and her cup was brought to her and taken away when she had finished drinking from it. Nobles entered as the main dinner of 24 dishes was set before her. There was a separate table for the nobles and this was served from the Queen's food platters once she herself was finished. Finally a basin was brought in for the Queen to wash her hands before she left. What is apparent from this account is the standardised ritualistic form that this meal took. However, as the Queen usually ate alone the public nature of this meal was unusual.

The second German account of Elizabeth dining comes 15 years later in 1599 and was observed by Thomas Platter. On this occasion the Queen was not in attendance at the main meal but rather in a separate room from the main company. Nevertheless, the same rituals were carried out, even though she was not present. Initially the trestle tables were carried into the room and laid with plates, knives, bread and the salt. Then the food was carried in with great ceremony, on 40 dishes, and laid out. Selections were cut off and carried through to the Queen in the adjoining room and only when she had finished dining was the rest distributed to the seated nobles, who had fresh dishes to eat from. Platter's description is very similar to that of von Wedel. What is more remarkable is that the rituals did not change whether the queen was in attendance or not. Platter specifically mentioned that the food bearers would bow to where the Queen would have been sitting, had she been in the room. Even though this was a dinner at the highest level it helps to demonstrate the potential hierarchical and inflexible nature of elite dining in general during this period. Moreover this was a use of the meal as an instrument of pure political theatre, with the observers, such as von Wedel, forming a willing and eager audience.

John Stow describes a further feast, dating to the reign of Henry VIII. It is different from the above accounts, as it was held in Goldsmith's Hall by the Lord Mayor of London. In attendance were both French ambassadors and English nobles, a total of around 100 people. They were seated at three large tables and served by the group, each referred to as a 'mess'. Stow records that for the whole feast there were a total of 15 messes, that is there were roughly seven people eating at each mess. During the dinner three courses were served and cleared, the first consisting of 15 silver dishes to each mess, the second 12 parcel gilt dishes and the third 10 full gilt dishes. In total each mess of seven people received 37 dishes, so the entire dinner required 555 silver, parcel and full gilt dishes. Not only was the quantity of food required for this feast staggering, but also the amount of flatware required to serve it. If Stow is to be believed all the silver and gilt was new, and freshly engraved with the Lord Mayor's personal mark. This account shows not only the considerable quantity of vessels required for this particular meal, but also the complexity of the ritual, with its divisions into material types for courses and numbers to a mess. Such enormous services of silver are far from the fancies of

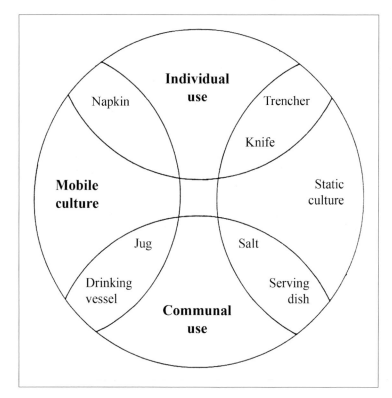

51 Schematic representation of the various classes of material culture used in dining

contemporary observers. One surviving example is the so-called Armada Service, dating to 1581-1601, which consists of 26 (although there were probably originally more) platters, plates and bowls. Belonging to Sir Christopher Harris, it gives the impression of the scale of bullion that a provincial Admiralty official could accrue (52). Therefore, as with the royal dinners of Elizabeth I, the Lord Mayor of London was using the spectacle of his feast, and particularly the extensive range of silver gilt tablewares, to impress both those dining and the assembled onlookers.

Whilst these three meals were all of a largely ceremonial nature, both von Wedel and Platter also comment on smaller, more ordinary meals, but still in the households of the rich. When dining at the residence of the governor of Berwick upon Tweed in 1584, von Wedel notes that, although he was well treated, there was no silver used at the table, only tin dishes and wooden plate. Similarly Platter when dining with the sword bearer of the Lord Mayor of London in 1599 described a smaller-scale meal. First their hands were washed with scented waters and the Grace was said. The diner's bowls, made of pewter, were each individually taken and filled with meat by the carver before being returned. There was still a great variety of foods and wines, although there was none of the theatre that he had previously witnessed at Elizabeth's dinner.

52 Part of the 'Armada Service' parcel-gilt dishes 1581-1601

Although material culture is only briefly mentioned in these (and other) descriptions of dining, they still serve as important indications of how the table operated. On the most basic level the way vessels were used around the table can be seen. What emerges are several classes of artefact, those intended for individual and communal use, which could be either static or mobile in operation. Initially, when the diner approached the table, an array of vessels was already present. Before each person were static items intended for exclusive personal use, a trencher of bread or wood and a knife. There were also static items shared communally between a 'mess' or group of people. These included serving platters, dishes and the salt (51).

Other vessels were mobile and could be used both on a communal and an individual basis. Both Platter and von Wedel mention the ritual of washing hands with water poured from a common ewer into a basin at the start of the meal. Likewise drinking vessels did not normally sit at the table, but on the cupboard. From here they were filled and brought to the table to be taken away once drunk from and cleaned ready for the next user. Although this seems to be a development away from the medieval idea of a communal cup, where everyone drank from a single vessel passed around the table, the individual diners did not yet have their own vessel. Finally certain items of material culture were mobile, but intended for personal use and hygiene. Napkins and bowls for the discard of waste food from the mouth could be brought to the individual diner when required and then removed, but were never shared between guests.

On a secondary level, these accounts of dining reflect the wider societal values of the period. Concepts of hierarchy and status were confirmed through the seating plan and order of service. The physical layout and the vessels used carried hidden messages. In a similar fashion the rituals enacted at the meals of Queen Elizabeth, even when she was not present, helped emphasise her regal power and the legitimacy of her position. It is all the more interesting that both Platter and von Wedel were allowed to observe these goings-on, even if they were not allowed to partake. Their descriptions indicate that the Crown was keen for outsiders to observe these rituals of power.

Similar messages were given at the Lord Mayor's Goldsmith's Hall feast. Here the assembled French ambassadors and English nobles were treated to a display of the new Lord Mayor's wealth. The cost of the food, added to the enormous quantity of bullion used, would have left an important impression. Clearly, this was carefully stage-managed, with the use of increasingly more magnificent dishes with each course intended to create amazement. It is not hard to imagine why the Lord Mayor also went to great pains to make sure that his personal mark or emblem was displayed on all the plate.

Through these more exotic manifestations of the meal it is easy to lose sight of the ritualistic aspects of more ordinary dining. Even as foreigners, both Platter and von Wedel were received into people's homes for more domestic meals. Both give accounts of smaller-scale events and their concern is not so much with the grandeur or demonstration of power as with common hospitality. The meal was a chance for the host to show their generosity and kindness by making their home open to passing visitors. Meals were a time when more informal loyalties could be made and these were not so influenced by the vessels on the table. Von Wedel is still honoured by the governor of Berwick, despite the tin dishes and wooden plates. Indeed it can be seen that at the beginning of the Tudor dynasty the use of base metals was thought appropriate for use even in the Royal Household. Pewter plates, and bowls, found in a hoard at Guy's Hospital in London in 1899, were stamped with the ostrich feather and are attributed to Arthur Prince of Wales, who died in 1503 (53). Often it was not the material that tablewares were made from that was important, but the way that they were used.

THE MATERIALS OF DINING

Several contemporary accounts of dining have been discussed above outlining some of the impressions, particularly of formalised state meals, gained by outside observers. There are certain problems in relying solely on some of the accounts of larger scale meals that were clearly stage-managed and intended to impress.

53 Pewter dish with the ostrich feather of Arthur Prince of Wales, 1485-1503

However, the Tudor meal cannot be viewed as either innovative or a static ritual, rather it was a continuing process that evolved from later medieval origins, particularly in terms of both the numbers of vessels present and the ways that they were used.

Household accounts of the fifteenth and sixteenth centuries give a good impression of many of the foodstuffs consumed, particularly by elite groups. Those who could afford them ate stews, fish and roasted meats in relatively large quantities. Food and drink was always prepared away from the table and then brought to the hall to be consumed by the assembled diners, who ate in a communal fashion. Less clear from such inventories are the relative numbers of vessels used at the table and the way that they operated between the diners.

Contemporary depictions provide one of the clearest views of the progress of the medieval meal. Those shown at the meal usually have a wooden or bread trencher in front of them, and help themselves to food from communal dishes. Drinking vessels were sparse on the table, a situation that was still the case in 1500 when a Venetian observed that the English did not consider it 'any inconvenience for three or four individuals to drink out of the same cup'. Although many of the more complex aspects of material culture for use at the table may have been established during the medieval period, it was not until the sixteenth and seventeenth centuries that a more distinctive and personalised 'table-set' appears in contemporary illustrative and descriptive accounts of dining in Northern Europe.

During the sixteenth century in England there were an increasing number of artefacts at the table. There was a general trend towards, but not yet a complete formalisation of, individual place settings and tablewares for each diner. One of the few depictions of English feasting from this period is of Sir Henry Unton, painted shortly after his death in 1596 (*colour plate 12*). This shows some evolution of the dining process from the medieval situation. At the table every guest had their own individual plate and there were larger numbers of dishes from which each person could help themself. However, as yet there were no drinking vessels placed on the table itself.

Despite many of the continuing medieval traditions in dining, new artefact forms were adopted in the sixteenth and subsequent centuries. Whereas previously guests might bring their own knives and eat with their fingers, implements were now provided at the table and these increasingly included spoons and less than a century later forks. Certainly by the later sixteenth century once functional vessels had become elaborate decorative table centrepieces. The presence of expensive silver gilt salts, colourful Maiolica dishes and decorative glasses from this period, demonstrates that not all the material culture at the table was purely functional. It is clear that with an increasingly complex and regulated dining process both the roles of dining and the material culture associated with it were changing.

TABLEWARES AND THE EXPRESSION OF TASTE

In 1674 Robert's *L'Art de Bien Traiter*, an instruction manual described in its title as being 'useful to all people and conditions', explained the importance of presentation of food dishes, due to:

> the politeness and propriety of their service, their quantity in proportion to the number of people, and finally the general order of things which contribute essentially to the quality and beauty of a meal that charms both the palate and the eye.

The expression of refinement and taste was felt not only to be within the food on the table, but also in the manner of its presentation. When this passage was written the way that the meal affected both the palate and, more importantly, the eye was a consideration. It has already been noted that during the sixteenth century there was an increasingly complex dining ritual, reflected in greater numbers of material objects at use on the table. This may in part be due to increased affluence and availability of luxury goods. However, these factors aside, it is probable that there was a genuine demand for larger numbers of new goods, to enable the increased demonstration of ideas of taste.

It is commonly observed that within sixteenth-century Europe there was a rapid increase in the use of certain highly decorative ceramic forms, such as Maiolica (*colour plate 13*). An explanation can be found in the desire for new decorative goods; Maiolica also fitted this new niche in the market. A similar argument for the increased importation of Germanic stonewares into England can be suggested, particularly in the light of the occasional exotic gilt mounts applied to them once they had arrived. However for the purpose of this chapter a single specific case study of glass will be taken.

By the end of the fifteenth century, there was virtually no use of glass tablewares in England. However during the sixteenth century glass, like Maiolica and stonewares, became increasingly popular, initially through imported and then domestically produced vessels. An insight into the renewed desire for glass can be seen in Harrison's oft quoted statement:

> It is a world to see in these our daies, wherin gold and silver most aboundeth, how that our gentilitie as lothing those mettals (bicause of the plentie) do now generallie choose rather the Venice glasses, both for our wine and beere.

He suggests this was because it was 'the nature of man generallie, that it most coveteth things difficult to be atteind'. To what extent gold and silver 'aboundeth' is unclear in the late sixteenth century, however Harrison suggests that glass was popular due to its scarcity. The import of the new luxury item at great expense clearly demonstrated the awareness and longing for the latest fashions. During the sixteenth century glass fitted a stylish niche amongst the elite, a fact attested to by its presence archaeologically on high status sites of this period.

Glass was just one medium that became increasingly popular at this time, and yet it encapsulates many of the contemporary concepts of design and metaphor shared by ceramics and metalwares. Ideally all aspects of dining culture should be examined together, so that we can begin to understand these meanings and metaphors. The lack of archaeological survival of many elements, both material and cultural, coupled with necessities of specialised artefact study makes this a difficult aim to accomplish. Given this, a very specific example can be used to emphasise the importance of this approach.

THE EXCLUSIVITY OF DESIGN: A GROUP OF ENGRAVED GLASS GOBLETS

Glass goblets (or stemmed wares) were a popular form of communal drinking vessel, primarily for wine, from the late twelfth to the fourteenth centuries, where their forms often broadly echoed metalwares and ecclesiastical chalices in particular. From the late fourteenth century they are found in fewer numbers when beakers become more popular; and they are largely absent from most assemblages dating to the end of that century. However, during the second half of the sixteenth century, with the revival of the domestic glass industry and increasing importation from abroad, goblets rapidly became one of the most common form of drinking vessel.

The reasons for the flourishing numbers of glass goblets at this time mainly remain speculative, but the glass goblet was a very visible symbol at the table. This is in part due to the fact that the goblet was a more conspicuous item than other forms, such as beakers, standing on a raised and decorative stem. Furthermore, as a goblet was a vessel that could be used communally, most diners would have seen it at close quarters, even if they did not drink from it. As an important symbol the goblet was the ideal object for the display of the most conspicuous imagery used to express social metaphors of taste and status. In an attempt to decipher some of these messages the most distinctive and costly mode of goblet decoration, diamond engraving, is considered here.

Diamond engraving first emerged in the middle of the sixteenth century, where it probably originated in Venice, certainly Vincenzo di Angelo dal Gallo applied for a patent to protect this technique there in 1549. This style of decoration consisted of scoring the outlines figural or floral motifs, which were subsequently hatched-in with small diagonal strokes. Other typical embellishments were bands of scrollwork and enclosed cartouches or heraldic devices. By the later sixteenth and seventeenth centuries, diamond engraving was practised at many other European glassmaking centres. Nevertheless, the technique was the most time consuming and expensive mode of decoration and it is not surprising that such vessels are correspondingly rare in England.

The study of diamond engraved glass in England has in the past concentrated exclusively on the attribution of complete museum pieces to the late sixteenth-century London workshop of Giacomo Verzelini. The engraver Anthony de Lysle was recorded as working in England at this time, suggesting that the diamond engraving could be ascribed to him. There are 10 engraved vessels traditionally attributed to the workshop of Verzelini and one to his successor Sir Jerome Bowes. However, archaeology has provided increasing numbers of examples, which are also worthy of consideration.

Many of the decorative motifs on these vessels are very similar, and can be broadly grouped into three stylistic themes. The first is the depiction of hunting, usually with deer being chased by dogs through a woodland scene. Four intact glasses decorated in this way are preserved in museum collections and they all have dates engraved on them ranging between 1577-81, as well as cartouches incorporating sets of owner's initials. Perhaps one of the most interesting of these, dated 1577 and with the owners' initials RB & IB was broken in the seveteenth century and had a replacement wooden foot made (54).

The second category of engraved vessels is those with simple floral designs that can incorporate geometric shapes such as ovals and borders of scrollwork. Two complete examples of this variety, one dated 1580, have been identified. The final type of decoration is the engraving of banded mottoes, usually just below the rim of the vessel (discussed in greater detail below). These are all in English, suggesting that they were at least decorated here. A particularly fine example of one of these is the 'KY' glass, now in the Corning Museum of glass, which also, interestingly, has a broken foot with a contemporary repair (55).

Given potential problems with the possible provenance of these museum pieces (some may never have actually been used in England), it is important that the further group of engraved vessels found archaeologically be considered. Thirteen diamond engraved vessels have now been recovered from archaeological contexts. These came from ten different sites, and, with two exceptions, all were found in central and south-eastern England.

The most complete archaeological example of an engraved vessel so far recovered came from a pit at Minster House in St Lawrence Poultney Lane, London (56). It consisted of a complete base, gilt ribbed inverted baluster stem and a tazza bowl, of which half still survives. The bowl was decorated with a hunt scene containing of two or three hounds and a stag, all in a wooded setting. This was bordered above and below with bands of running scrollwork and had a teardrop design radiating out close to the stem. Fragments from two other goblets baring hunting scenes, although with u-shaped bowls, have also been found at Southampton (57).

The remaining archaeological glasses are simpler in design and only consist of panels or borders of floral and geometric designs. A goblet bowl from Cheapside, London has only foliate border and looped design above, but despite the simplicity of its design is very finely engraved (58 (top)). A fragmentary goblet bowl recovered from Blomfield Street, also in London, was decorated with floral and geometric patterns of a more complex nature (58 (middle)). The engraving can be divided into three zones. The upper contained alternating teardrops and vertical loops, above a horizontal band of running scrollwork. The middle zone seems to be comprised only of a foliage pattern, again separated from the

54 Engraved hunt scene goblet 1577

55 Engraved floral scene 'KY' goblet 1583

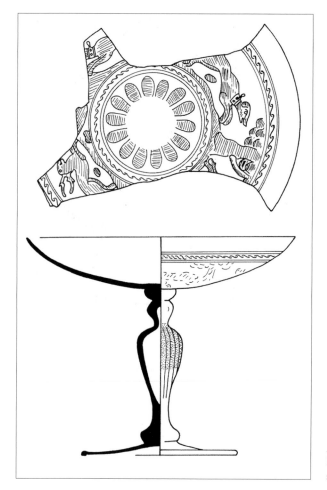

56 Engraved tazza, Minster
House, London. Last quarter
sixteenth century

lower zone by a band of horizontal running scrolls. This lower zone was the
mirror image of the upper, with reversed teardrops and vertical loops. A third
goblet with foliage design comes from Wood Hall, although the engraving was
restricted to around its rim and consists of a floral and leaf design, with a running
scroll border above (58 (bottom)). Small fragments of similar glasses with scroll
and foliage design also come from Oxford; Camber Castle (Sussex); Sheffield
Manor (Yorks) and Nonsuch Palace (Surrey). Three other fragments of engraved
glass, from Acton Court (Avon); Canterbury (Kent) and Chelmsford (Essex), are
all too small for positive identification.

57 Two engraved goblets from Southampton, 1580s

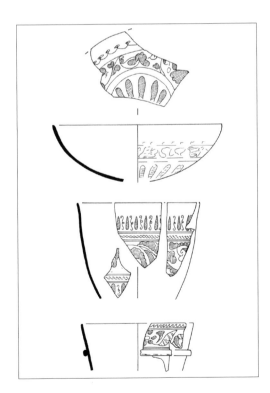

58 Floral engraved goblets from (top) Cheapside, London, (middle) Blomfield Street, London, (bottom) Wood Hall, Yorks

UNDERLYING METAPHORS: ENGRAVED GLASS AND ITS SOCIAL SIGNIFICANCE

Despite the fact that there are some problems in the attribution of manufacturing provenance to some of these engraved vessels, it is clear that such highly decorated and costly vessels appealed to a certain section of Tudor society. The obvious fragility of glass in part explains this, as an investment in glass was a demonstration of conspicuous consumption and wealth. However, what also might have made these vessels appeal to a contemporary audience are the implicit and explicit messages that they bore through their design.

Engraved vessels were clearly high-status objects for a number of reasons, the most apparent being that engraving was only carried out on the highest quality vessels. This might appear to be an obvious association, but it is not necessarily the case. The technology required to score the surface of the glass was extremely simple. Although it is supposed that a diamond tipped instrument was used for the high quality vessels, there was no practical reason why other hard substances, such as quartz, could not have been. Despite this, no engraving ever occurs on poorer quality vessels in England. This is not to say that the highly complex motifs and design should be expected on potash or poor quality mixed alkali glass, but it would not have been a complex process to apply simple geometric designs or horizontal bands to these vessels. The complete absence of engraved or incised decoration on any but the top grade of glass suggests that it was only considered appropriate to them.

The exclusivity of this decoration can be further indicated by consideration of the method of its execution. Although it is not certain how long it would have taken the craftsman to engrave a complete goblet bowl, in proportion to the time required to create the vessel it was considerably greater. The process of blowing a three-part goblet would only have taken a few minutes, even if it were decorated with other features, such as trailing. The investment of time to engrave a glass completely would have incurred considerable extra expense.

By the nature of their decoration, engraved glasses were capable of carrying the most evocative imagery. Such engraved vessels demonstrate the only form of decoration used on glass, with the possible exception of enamelling, where the customer directly influenced the imagery. This can be seen most obviously by the presence of cartouches of owner's initials, an element that had to be applied upon special request. Such an example can be seen on the KY glass, where not only could the customer have their initials added, but also more complex ciphers (59). Consequently diamond engraving allowed the purchaser, and user, to 'tailor make' the vessel decoration specifically to their own requirements. As with personalised cartouches the purchaser could apparently specify the inclusion of specific mottoes and probably was able to choose the stylised scenes that appeared on the vessel. This control over the decoration allowed the customer to imbue the vessel with messages far more personalised than any other form of decoration.

The examination of the different styles reveals a variety of social messages. The most obvious of these were hunting scenes. Examples fall into two broad categories. The first consists of a panel of several hounds chasing a stag, against a backdrop of trees and foliage. Example of this decoration can be seen on both complete vessels (e.g. 54) and archaeological glasses, such as the tazza from Minster House, London (56). The second variation on this theme occurred on three of the complete historic vessels and one of the archaeological fragments from Southampton (57 (a)). As well as the hunt scene with stag and hounds, these examples also include a unicorn within the decorative running panel.

The imagery on these glasses was symbolic of a high-status elite pursuit. An allusion to hunting on these vessels suggests that the users wished to associate

59 Detail of cipher on the 'KY' goblet 1583

themselves with 'the chase', even if they did not actually participate. Only the wealthy could afford to hunt and by displaying such obvious images on a glass the owner was making an expressive statement. The inclusion of unicorns within this decorative motif further enhanced the theme. According to myth no hunter, however skilful, could capture the unicorn. Thus the inclusion of the animal as an elusive quarry fitted in with the general genre.

Personalised cartouches and mottoes were a further dimension of this symbolism. Nine of the intact historic glasses bore either groups of owners' initials or mottoes in English and often a combination of the two. The use of initials or even full names was clearly intended to enhance the prestige of the vessel and its owner, as was the inclusion of the Royal Arms of Queen Elizabeth I on one example. The use of mottoes appears to have been intended to strengthen further particular relationships. Some can be seen as familial, 'To his brother Richard Grenal', on one glass, whilst others were obvious displays of loyalty to the Crown, 'God save Quyne Elizabeth' for example. Finally overt religious sentiments could be expressed in this way, with two of the intact glasses carrying the identical motto '*In God is al miy trvst*' (60).

Whilst all of the intact vessels fall into these categories, it would appear that many excavated fragments do not bear any surviving hunt scenes, cartouches or mottoes. In these cases, the decoration seems to consist entirely of foliage designs and scrollwork. With such vessels it is harder to identify the overt messages. However, the presence of engraved decoration alone may have been sufficient to convey certain meanings to the user.

One of the most striking features of complete vessels was that their manufacture and use was seemingly restricted to the last quarter of the sixteenth century. This would also seem to be the case with the fragmented archaeological examples, where the contextual dating is sufficiently refined to allow such conclusions to be drawn. Only one of the dated glasses falls into the seventeenth century, having been engraved in 1602. This contrasts with the situation in the rest of Europe, where diamond engraved glass continued to be produced and used with increasing frequency throughout the seventeenth century. Further, engraving in the Netherlands during the seventeenth century increasingly occurred on poorer quality potash and mixed alkali vessels, predominately glass roemers, suggesting that it was extending further down the social scale.

However, this was never the case in England and the production and consumption of engraved glass seems to have ceased by the early seventeenth century. The reasons for this cessation in engraving are probably connected to wider aspects of glass use. By the seventeenth century glass as a medium was extending far further down the social scale, compared to the preceding century when high quality vessels are only found on elite sites such as castles and manors.

60 Engraved goblet, IN:GOD:IS:AL:MY:TRVST 1586

Archaeologically glass is increasingly found on more urban 'middling' sites, whilst the reverse is true on elite sites where it appears to lose its exclusivity. Against these wider trends the expensive processes of engraving could not and did not survive. The elite were seeking new items of different media for their cultural expressions, whilst those lower down the social scale still could not afford such a costly decorative device.

CONCLUSION

Through the examination of contemporary accounts from Tudor England, a partial picture of dining, at least at the higher levels of society, emerges. The accounts of Platter and von Wedel, who interestingly were allowed and encouraged to observed the proceedings, show that dining was a highly formalised affair and actively used to reinforce political and social messages at court. Strict hierarchies were supported by the order of service, and the specific nature of the rituals undertaken. It is clear that public meals at court were strictly stage-managed, and it is striking that there is little variance whether or not the Queen was in attendance. Many of these same rituals were also observed in more informal and less courtly settings. Hand washing, the formalised use of napkins and the steady procession of different dishes were also observed by both Platter and von Wedel in the houses of private individuals. Whilst it is clear that the food and the spatial setting were prime elements in dining, objects and tablewares also played a crucial role.

On one hand tablewares were very necessary on purely a functional level, particularly against the background of the growing culinary sophistication occurring during the Tudor period. Increasing numbers of dishes and plates, as well as more personalised elements such as knives and spoons, were required to deal with the greater variety of food that appeared on the table. However, it is clear from other dining accounts that tablewares played a more sophisticated role too. John Stow's account of the feast of the Lord Mayor of London is revealing. The use of increasingly more impressive silver, parcel gilt and gilt dishes for each course was clearly designed as a visual effect. Likewise the Lord Mayor used the dishes as an impressive backdrop for the display of his own freshly applied mark or emblem. In this context the self-promotional aspect of the tableware is obvious.

The use of tablewares made from precious metals was an obvious way to display messages of wealth and social status. However, there were also many more subtle and sophisticated ways that other vessel types could be used to the same end. One such class of artefact was drinking glasses, and goblets in particular.

Given that they would have originally cost a fraction of their silver equivalents, the growing popularity of glasswares during the sixteenth century suggest that there was the desire to display more than just physical wealth. One element of glass that might have appealed is the obvious conspicuous consumption of wealth by any investment in glass. Harrison observed in 1587 that glasses 'in time, all go one waie, that is, to shards at the last, so that our great expenses in glasses ... are worst of all bestowed in my opinion, bicause their peeces doo turne unto no profit'. He criticises the use of glass noting that once broken it lost all value, but perhaps he is missing the point. It is because of this that glass might have appealed, any guest using such a fragile item would have been fully aware of their host's precarious investment.

There was also a further dimension to the use of glass, which was also shared by other tableware media that were becoming increasingly popular at an elite level, as well as further down the social scale. The development of highly decorative wares in ceramic and glass allowed a wider range of people to have access to fashionable and decorative goods for their tables. It was now possible for aspiring groups to obtain goods that reflected to the assembled guests their appreciation of the fashions and tastes of the period. Glass was eminently well-suited to this purpose. As has been shown in this chapter, the buyer was able to customise their tablewares to reflect their aspirations and feelings. With the engraved glasses it is probably no coincidence then, that courtly pursuits such as hunting were popular, as well as the allegorical use of the unicorn. In less elaborate ways, the use of personalised cartouches and mottoes also had a similar effect. It is clear that at most levels of society a crucial element in the theatre of Tudor dining was fulfilled by not only the objects on the table but also the materials they were made from and their decoration.

Hugh Willmott

ACKNOWLEDGEMENTS

I am grateful to Dawn Hadley and Maureen Carroll for comments on an earlier draft of this chapter. The following institutions gave permission for the reproduction of images: The Corning Museum of Glass, New York (figs 54, 55 and 59); The British Museum (*colour plate 12*); and The National Portrait Gallery, London (*colour plate 13*). The remaining photographs are by the author.

BIBLIOGRAPHY

Ariès, P., and Duby, G., (eds) *A History of Private Life vol. 3 Passions of the Renaissance* (Harvard, 1988)

Brett, G., *Dinner is Served; A History of Dining in England 1400-1900* (London, 1968)

von Bülow, G., 'Journey through England & Scotland made by Lupold von Wedel in the years 1584 & 1585', *Transactions of the Royal Historical Society*, new series IX (1895), pp.223-70

Byrne, M. St Clare., (ed.) *The Elizabethan Home, Discovered in Two Dialogues by Claudius Hollyband and Peter Erondell*, 2nd ed (London, 1930)

Chartier, R,. 'From text to manners. A concept and its books: civilité between aristocratic distinction and popular appropriation', in L.Cochrane (ed.), *The Cultural Uses of Print in Early Modern France* (Princeton University Press, 1987), pp.71-109

Elias, N., *The Civilising Process; Vol. 1 The History of Manners* (Oxford, 1978)

Hammond, P., *Food and Feast in Medieval England* (Stroud, 1993)

Harrison, W., *The Description of England* (New York, 1994)

Jeanneret, M., *A Feast of Words, Banquets and table talk in the Renaissance* (Cambridge, 1991)

Lethbridge-Kingsford, C., (ed.) *John Stow's a Survey of London, vols. 1 and 2* (Oxford, 1908)

Sim, A., *Food and Feast in Tudor England* (Stroud, 1997)

Sneyd, C., *A Relation, or Rather a True Account, of the Island of England; with sundry particulars of the customs of these people, and of the royal revenues under King Henry the Seventh about the year 1500* (Camden Society 1st series 37, 1847)

Williams, C., (ed.) *Thomas Platter's Travels in England 1599* (London, 1937)

nine

LUNCH AT THE TOPKAPI PALACE: THE ARCHAEOLOGY OF THE TABLE DURING OTTOMAN TIMES

Turkish cuisine is often considered as an *haute cuisine*, based on a highly developed courtly society and social competition. In this perspective it ranks among the Chinese, Indian and French cuisines. Being influenced by Persian, Chinese and Middle Eastern flavours, Turkish cuisine attained its height during the Ottoman period (roughly the fifteenth to nineteenth centuries AD). Today, quite a lot is known about the culinary aspects of the Turkish elite in this period because visitors from the West described the eating habits at the Ottoman court. In fact, these foreigners often described the table customs at the Topkapi Palace in more detail than the residents, because as outsiders they were in a position to record what was 'peculiar' (to them) in the Ottoman etiquette and culinary conventions.

This chapter attempts to catch a glimpse of wining and dining habits at the Ottoman court in Constantinople (modern Istanbul) as seen through the eyes of such an outsider, the eighteenth-century ambassador of the Dutch Republic, Cornelis Calkoen. In addition, it deals with the Ottoman rules of etiquette relating to eating and drinking, often derived from Islamic doctrine, and in a wider sense it deals with the development of dining manners in the Ottoman Empire from the late fifteenth to the eighteenth centuries. All this is approached from an archaeological perspective. Therefore, special emphasis is put on the material aspects of Turkish cuisine, in particular the dining equipment in the Imperial kitchens of the Topkapi Palace at Istanbul. Here, Chinese porcelains, silverware and locally produced tin-glazed ceramics (such as Iznik and Kütahya Ware) were stored in large quantities. Palace kitchen records and Ottoman miniatures give some idea of how these high-quality wares were used during sumptuous banquets.

61 Portrait of the Dutch ambassador Cornelis Calkoen (1696–1764) by Jean–Baptiste Vanmour.
Amsterdam, Rijksmuseum A-1996

CORNELIS CALKOEN VISITS THE TOPKAPI PALACE

On Sunday, 14 September 1727, the ambassador of the Dutch Republic, Cornelis Calkoen, had the honour of being received in audience at the Ottoman court by Sultan Ahmed III. Calkoen made an extensive description of this special visit to the Sultan and his son-in-law, the grand vizier Damad Ibrahim Pasha. This report is now in the State archives in The Hague and will here be referred to as the 'Relaes'.

Cornelis Calkoen was born on 21 May 1696 in Amsterdam into a wealthy patrician's family engaged in trade with the Levant (61). Ironically, the family name means literally 'a turkey' in Dutch. Known as a friendly gentleman of an enormous stature, he was ambassador of the Dutch Republic at the Porte in Constantinople from 1725 until 1743. Apparently, he owed this post to the efforts of a relative, Amsterdam's mayor Jan Six, who belonged to the well-known Dutch Six-dynasty so often painted by Rembrandt in the seventeenth century. As a diplomat, Cornelis Calkoen was not particularly successful, but his personality and stature seemed to appeal to the imagination of future generations. Long after his death in 1764 there were many rumours about him and his beautiful mistress, a freed slave known as Beyaz Gul ('White Rose'). Eventually, the stories found a literary epitome in the historical novel Grand Seigneur, written by M.C. van Zeggelen, with Calkoen as the leading character.

Cornelis Calkoen not only wrote a detailed report about his audience at the court of Ahmed III to his principals (the Bureau of Levantine Trade in Amsterdam), he also desired a painted account of this important event. To that end he commissioned the French painter Jean-Baptiste Vanmour (1671-1737), who was noted for his realistic and truthful audience-pictures made for several French ambassadors and a Swedish diplomat in the early eighteenth century. In fact, Vanmour's work was becoming so famous among Constantinople's diplomatic circles that the increasing amount of orders forced him to found a 'school' with assistants.

Vanmour painted three pictures of Calkoen's audience to the Topkapi Palace. All three give interesting information concerning the ceremony of an ambassadorial visit to the Ottoman court. On the first painting (Rijksmuseum A-4076) the Dutch ambassador can be seen with his entourage crossing the enormous second courtyard of the Topkapi Palace, some 130m long and 110m wide (62 (3)), while a thousand soldiers of the Sultan's standing army, the so-called Janissaries, were eating from dishes (also known as çanak yağması or 'pot plundering') (63). According to the 'Relaes' the Janissaries happily devoured a few loaves of bread and dishes with boiled rice (pilav), which Calkoen interpreted as solemn proof of their loyalty and submission to the Sultan.

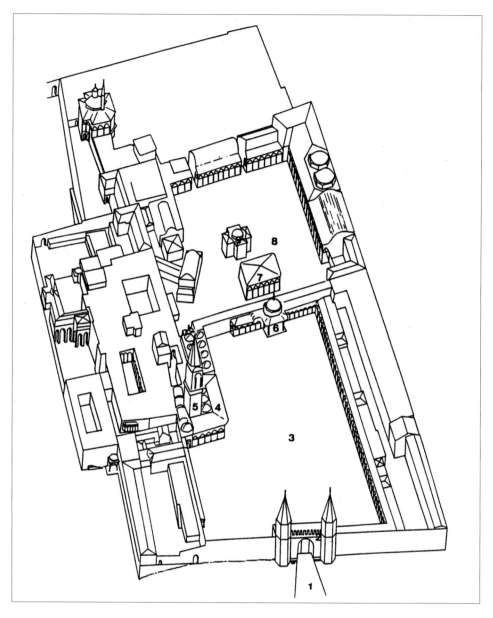

62 Drawing of the Topkapi Palace in Istanbul

Vanmour's second painting (Rijksmuseum A-4077) is even more revealing, because it depicts the lunch presented to Calkoen by the grand vizier in the name of Sultan Ahmed III (*colour plate 14*). The Dutch ambassador was received by the grand vizier inside the Council Hall or Divan (*62* (4)), after which food was served from the palace kitchens as a gesture of the Sultan's hospitality

63 Painting of ambassador Cornelis Calkoen and his entourage crossing the second courtyard of the Topkapi Palace by Jean-Baptiste Vanmour. *Amsterdam, Rijksmuseum A-4076*

towards his official guests. Around three sides of the room there was a low couch covered with Turkish carpets (the Divan from which the council took its name). The 'Relaes' gives a detailed description of the event. Calkoen sat on a stool, next to two interpreters. The meal was presented on low wooden stands that were covered with large round trays, made of silver, to serve as tables during the meal. On these trays pieces of bread and spoons, made of ivory or ebony, were put down for each diner. The food was served in large bowls, which were placed in the centre of the tray. Everyone had to eat communally with his fingers from the same dish: 'which was taken away so fast that one is only able to put one's hand in it no more than two or three times'. Calkoen was also astonished by the fact that his hosts did not use any plates or napkins. After the meal, which lasted for no more than half an hour, the diners washed their hands and drank coffee.

Finally, on Vanmour's third painting (Rijksmuseum A-4078) Calkoen's actual audience with Sultan Ahmed III can be seen (65). The foreign envoy was taken through the Gate of Felicity into the Throne Room in the third court, where he was presented to the Sultan (62 (7)). The most important event for an ambassador was his first audience with the Sultan, a kind of initiation-ritual with a great

64 Painting of ambassador Cornelis Calkoen in audience with Sultan Ahmed III by Jean-Baptiste Vanmour. *Amsterdam, Rijksmseum A-4078*

show of strength of the Sultan's standing army, the Janissaries, where the envoy received humiliation as well as accolades.

DINING HABITS AT THE OTTOMAN COURT

Formal banquets at the Ottoman court offered to ambassadors from Western Europe revealed more than just the table customs in the Topkapi Palace. The degree of lavishness of the banquet was also a reflection of the relative status of the persons being honoured. The longer the meal lasted, the higher the visitor was regarded by the Sultan. However, the meals were not only for the benefit of the foreign envoys. At the same time dishes with food were offered to the complete court entourage (including the Janissaries in the second court). This ostentatious public feeding was an important part of the court ceremonial, stressing the corporate unity of the palace household and its dependency on the Sultan.

In the eighteenth century, when Cornelis Calkoen was received in audience by the Sultan, the visitor was offered a meal immediately before his presentation to the Sultan. However, three centuries earlier the order of ceremony was the

65 Picture of a so-called *sini* with metal dishes on top

other way round. Initially, it was the Ottoman custom to offer a banquet to the foreign envoys directly after their official audience with the Sultan. The first description of such a dinner was written by the French knight Bertrandon de la Brocquière in 1433. According to de la Brocquière, all the guests sat on the ground and ate from a round thin cloth made of leather (a so-called *sofra*). On this were placed metal dishes filled with rice and meat. Curiously, the meal did not include bread or drink. The host, Sultan Murad II (1421-51), was the only person who got a long silk cloth, a napkin and two big golden plates with meat. He was dining separately in the same room, but he was eating and drinking very little. It looked as if his presence at this dinner was more symbolic than to satisfy his appetite. Murad's successor to the throne, Sultan Mehmed II (1451-81), however, no longer wished to eat together with his subjects. He preferred to dine only in the company of persons 'of royal blood'. Since then, it was decided that all foreign ambassadors were presented with a meal by the grand vizier in the Council Hall (or Divan) before the official audience with the Sultan.

Another revolutionary change in the dining protocol of the Ottoman court was the introduction of a circular tray on a wooden stand (the so-called *sini*) (65). This kind of table in an Occidental fashion was imposed by Sultan Suleyman the

Magnificent in the sixteenth century. From this time on we learn that guests sat around these low circular trays and ate from communal dishes. The trays were not provided with plates, salt pots, knives or forks. A sixteenth-century foreign visitor rather bluntly remarked about the eating with fingers at the court: 'everything was just torn apart'. The only utensils used were serving ladles and soup spoons. Dishes were either set out together, regardless of ingredients, or served in quick succession. This style of serving was followed at all social levels; the only difference between the elite and the common man being the quantity and quality of textiles, utensils and ingredients. The food was usually brought to the table in large bowls, copper dishes, covered pans or lidded porcelain dishes, which were placed in the centre. Everyone used to eat with their spoons or fingers from the same dish.

The meal included mutton, roasted pigeons and chicken, and rice cooked in various ways. White, freshly baked bread, made of wheat, was also on the menu. Fish and beef, however, were never served. For dessert, fruit was served on porcelain plates, with a variety of sweetmeats. During the banquet only persons of the highest rank drank *sherbet*, sweetened water flavoured with rosewater or lemon; the rest had to slake their thirst with water. After the meal the diners washed their hands and drank coffee.

An additional banquet was served to lesser members of the ambassador's retinue, who were not deemed worthy to eat in the Council Hall. Their food was served outside in one of the courtyards of the palace. According to the sixteenth-century traveller Guillaume Postel, a long carpet was unrolled to accommodate the diners. The carpet was large enough to seat all those invited, and offered enough space for a great number of porcelain dishes. A large crowd of soldiers, Janissaries and other palace attendants assembled to gaze silent and motionless at the spectacle of the foreigners dining.

There were many rules of etiquette relating to food and eating during the Ottoman period, often derived from Islamic doctrine. These included washing the hands before and after meals, using three fingers to pass the food from dish to mouth, using two hands to break the bread, not smacking the lips, not looking at what your neighbour was eating, turning one's head away from the table when coughing or sneezing, not talking with food in the mouth. Mealtimes fitted in with the daily ritual of prayer and were of special importance within Islam, where the communal consumption of food is a recommended activity according to a *hadith*, which records that the Prophet remarked 'Eat together with your family, since communal meals are blessed'.

Spoons were of foremost importance for eating soup or compote, and they came in many shapes and sizes. Often they were kept in carved or painted wooden spoon holders or embroidered bags known as *kasiklik*. At the Ottoman court there was even a hierarchy in the use of spoons. A receipt from 1729 about the acquisition of spoons for the Sultan shows that there were spoons for 'normal' dishes such as soup and rice, as well as special spoons for compote, eggs and rose jam. These spoons for the elite were sometimes made from gold, silver, tortoiseshell, mother-of-pearl, or sandalwood (which was very expensive), and set with coral, ivory or even precious stones. Ottoman miniatures give some idea of how these spoons were used. At a banquet depicted in the *Surnâme* of Sultan Ahmed III, individual spoons are placed in front of each guest, while there is a large serving soup tureen at the centre of the table (*colour plate 15*). There was even an intricate etiquette of eating soup communally, whereby the right side of the spoon was only used to dish the broth up and the left side to eat from.

Palace registers often list the quantities of porcelain plates, earthenware bowls and metal dishes purchased for formal banquets at the Topkapi Palace. From one register we learn that each table was laid with 27 serving dishes, six pans and 14 trays. While some guests sat at tables for six or seven, and others for three or four people, there were also tables laid on the ground for 100 people each. In all 80,000 plates, bowls and dishes could be used.

During public banquets for the ambassadors in the Divan there was an old tradition of carrying the food in silver and porcelain dishes from the palace kitchens to the Sultan's private residence and to the Council Hall. In 1599 Baron Wenceslas Wratislaw described the ingenious way in which servants would file in carrying the food from the kitchen:

> First came about 200 cup-bearers, or servers ... who placed themselves in a row from the kitchen to the Sultan's apartment When it was dinner time, the superintendent of the kitchen brought from the cook a porcelain dish, and another covered dish, handed it to the waiter nearest him, he to a third, and so on till it came to the one who stood nearest to the Emperor's apartment. There, again, stood other chamberlains, and one handed it to another, till the viands were carried very quickly, and without the slightest noise or clatter, to the Emperor's table. (Cited in Necipoglu 1991:72)

In addition, a similar row was formed to the table where the Council and foreign ambassadors were eating.

THE IMPERIAL KITCHENS

The palace kitchens, which extended along the right side of the second court at the Topkapi Palace, formed a series of ten spacious chambers, each with a high dome and a conical chimney. The kitchen courtyard was separated from the second court by a steep wall above which arose the tall chimneys of the

66 Imperial Kitchens
in the Topkapi Palace

kitchens (*66*). At the north end of the narrow courtyard was the mosque of
the royal kitchens, a small building with three domes. Adjacent to it were the
confectionery kitchens (known as the *Helvahâne*), where fruit conserves, syrups
and sweets (such as *helva*) were made. The 10 kitchens, which had a staff of about
1,500, all served different purposes. There were different kitchens for the Sultan,
followed by those for the queen mother (*valide sultan*), for the chief black eunuch
and wives of the Sultan, for the female officials and servants of the harem, and
for the other classes of servants, officials and guards.

Since the sixteenth century there were at least 600 cooks at work in the palace
kitchens, assisted by a force of servants and 'taste before-hands'. They cooked

with products in season, often with complicated cooking methods. There was a growing tendency for luxurious foodstuffs. In 1527-28 the Ottoman court spent more than 2.3 million akçe on the imperial kitchens. One hundred and thirty-one years later, in 1669-70, the expenses of the palace kitchens had risen to the remarkable sum of 52.5 million akçe.

The kitchen complex also included a larder and a commissariat, where valuable ceramic tableware was stored. A number of documents contain references to the pottery store. Account books of 1527-29, for instance, mention the repair of this 'ceramics room (*oda-i çini*) near the imperial kitchens'. Here imported blue and white porcelain from China was apparently stored together with the brightly coloured local tin-glazed pottery from nearby Iznik (in north-western Anatolia). The Chinese and Iznik ceramic tableware used at the circumcision ceremonies of princes at the Hippodrome, Istanbul in 1582 were loaned out from the same storeroom.

Nevertheless, the Sultan's porcelains were better protected against earthquakes and fires than the less prestigious Iznik ceramics. Istanbul had many fires that ravaged the city from the mid-fifteenth to the late nineteenth centuries. This is one of the main reasons why so little Iznik pottery has survived to this day in Turkey. Furthermore, the Sultan's passion for Chinese porcelain meant that it was costly, highly esteemed and kept in well-protected cellars (so that there was very little in circulation). Thanks to this, the Topkapi Palace has now the world's biggest collection of porcelain after Peking and Dresden: 10,700 pieces (ranging from the thirteenth to eighteenth centuries) have survived to the present day and are nowadays exhibited in the Imperial kitchen complex. Unfortunately, not a trace of Iznik pottery remains in this collection. Iznik plates were evidently not good enough for the Sultan, who preferred to eat off silver or gold plates, or green Celadon, which was thought both to detect and neutralize poison. As a result of this, the nicest and most complete pieces of Iznik ware can now be seen in Western collections, such as at the Victoria and Albert and British Museums.

IZNIK WARE

The almost complete absence of Iznik pottery from the Topkapi Palace today, in contrast to the large quantities of Chinese porcelain surviving there, means that it is necessary to rely almost entirely on documentary references in order to establish whether, and to what extent, Iznik pottery was used at the Sultan's court, in particular, and in the rest of Ottoman Empire in general (67). Ottoman documents thus far examined consist of schedules of fixed prices, probate inventories and various palace registers such as treasury accounts, stocktaking records, sale registers, palace kitchen records and inventories of gifts. The earliest

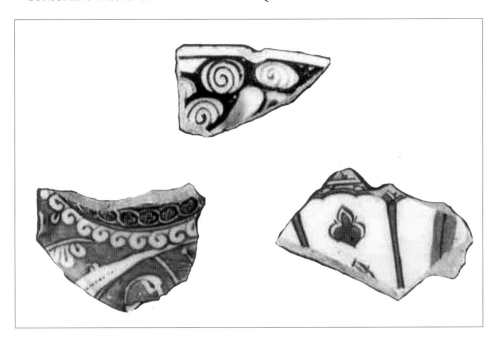

67 Fragments of Iznik ware, found at excavations in Greece

dated document mentioning Iznik ceramics in use at the Topkapi Palace can be dated in the year 1489-90. This register lists the types, quantities and prices of items, including Iznik pottery, purchased for the imperial kitchens. From this it is possible to learn that the cost of 97 Iznik vessels was at that time 1,916 akçe.

Another kitchen record from 1582 provides evidence that during special occasions (such as the festivities for the circumcision ceremonies of the son of Sultan Murad III, which lasted 52 days and nights), 541 extra Iznik plates, dishes and bowls were purchased from the bazaar, in addition to the Chinese porcelain, copperware and Iznik ceramics that were brought out of the Palace kitchens. According to Atasoy and Raby (1989), this suggests that a great deal of Iznik pottery was available on the open market, and that the Palace preferred to buy its Iznik vessels from the merchants in the Istanbul bazaar, rather than from the potters themselves.

Unlike foreign buyers, the Ottoman court paid fixed prices that were pegged to an artificially low scale for these wares. On an account from 1617-18 the prices of 6,331 types of Iznik ceramics range from 60-70 akçe for a large jar to only 2 akçe for a small cup. As a result, the Iznik potters increasingly preferred to make vessels for sale on the open market rather than ceramics on commission for the court. A royal decree sent to Iznik in 1585 ordered ceramic workshops to stop making tablewares for the open market and, instead turn their energies toward making tiles for the Topkapi Palace in Istanbul.

The documents also show that Iznik ware was mainly used as an everyday ware. Even in the sixteenth century, when the quality of fabric and decoration of Iznik ceramics reached its peak, the Ottoman Sultans preferred the more expensive and valuable foreign wares (such as Chinese porcelains). The archival sources suggest that Iznik ware was stored in large quantities in the Imperial kitchens of the Topkapi Palace, ready for use on a day-to-day basis. The documents refer to 'compote bowls', 'large yoghurt bowls', 'salad and sweetmeat dishes', 'lamb dishes', and even to 'dishes for various puddings' or 'for clotted cream'.

Prices and quantities in the probate inventories of Edirne's wealthy residents seem to indicate that, compared to Chinese porcelain, Iznik pottery was cheap and widely available. The potter's skill and the taste of the decoration made them an acceptable substitute for porcelain and for metal too. There is ample evidence for the importance of Iznik pottery in fine houses as opposed to vessels of wood, base metal (brass or copper), porcelains or even metal. It has rightly been suggested that at the Ottoman court Iznik ceramics perhaps filled the gap between wood, tinned copper or crude pottery kitchen wares on the one hand, and gold and silver on the other.

KÜTAHYA WARE

In the seventeenth and eighteenth centuries the potter's centre at Kütahya, about 200km southeast from Istanbul in north-western Anatolia, occupied the leading position held by Iznik in earlier periods. Pottery and tile manufacture had started here around the same time as in Iznik. Entries for 1444/5 and 1485/6 in the endowment registers for the Church of St Mary in Kütahya give the names of two potters, showing that potteries existed there already in the fifteenth century. The potters' workshops at Kütahya initially played a secondary role, providing Iznik with additional capacity when necessary. The fact that the Kütahya potteries were not dependent on court patronage enabled them to remain economically viable. From an imperial edict written to the *kadi* ('judge') of Kütahya in 1608 it is known that by this time there was even rivalry between the potters of Iznik and Kütahya. The kadi received instruction from Istanbul that the 'cup-makers of Kütahya' should sell soda to the chief tile maker in Iznik at the price set by the government.

Two government registers of fixed prices for the sale of various pottery have been published so far: one is dated 15 September 1600, the other 31 December 1640. The pottery recorded in the 1600 schedule is arranged by type. Under the heading of 'salad and sweetmeat dishes', the prices of pottery from Iznik and Kütahya are given (*68*). The list shows a puzzling (and as yet unexplained)

	New price	Old price
When they are Iznik	10	14
When they are Kütahya	8 or 7	16

68 New and old prices of Iznik and Kütahya wares in a 1600 AD

reversal, the older Kütahya dishes being more expensive, and the newer ones less expensive than Iznik.

Probate registers often list ceramics from Iznik and Kütahya together with Chinese porcelain in inventories of estates. They show that Iznik pottery is always valued lower than Chinese porcelain, although for one inventory of the possessions of one Haci Hürrem Bey, dated 1623, a piece of Chinese porcelain is valued at 150 akçe, compared to 60 akçe for an Iznik dish and 500 akçe for a Kütahya dish. The most distinctive products of Kütahya were thinly potted, polychrome painted vessels in a fine, whitish frit. Small coffee cups (often with matching saucers), bowls, jugs and coffee pots made up the majority of production (*69*). The shapes of the coffee cups were probably taken from Chinese porcelain or from porcelain made at Vienna and Meissen about 1730-40.

In the written sources of the time references to the use of this sort of coffee cup can be found. In 1839 the Western traveller Ami Boué described the serving of coffee in the Ottoman Empire, apparently referring to Kütahya ware: 'The coffee is served in very small cups made of porcelain ... which are often decorated with a fine golden rim, but only very rich people have them with painted decoration' (cited in Uksinus 1985:157). The delicacy of the Kütahya cups suggests that they were also made for intimate gatherings in Ottoman society, and not only for the robust public use in coffee houses and bazaars. Coffee drinking had become a form of national pastime in the eighteenth century. It was not only drunk in coffee houses, but also in the harem, in the bath-house (hamam) and at garden parties and picnics.

Remarks on the consumption of coffee are frequent in Lady Mary Wortley Montagu's famous Turkish letters, written while she accompanied her husband on a trip in 1718. She reported that after the end of meals she was often offered coffee served in small cups of 'the finest China with soucoups of silver gilt or gold'. There were sets of metal coffee pots, porcelain cups in filigree holders, and small dishes for offering coffee and refreshments to the guests. It has therefore been suggested that in the early eighteenth century Kütahya ware well suited the pleasure-seeking, romantic atmosphere that prevailed among the wealthy classes during the 'Tulip Age' of the Ottoman Empire.

Lemon-squeezers were also made at Kütahya in the first quarter of the eighteenth century. Lemons were not grown in northern Turkey, but we learn from various sources that lemons and lemon juice were imported from the

69 Fragments of Kütahya ware, found at excavations in Greece

Aegean to Istanbul in the seventeenth and eighteenth centuries for making lemon *sherbet*. This drink was a mixture of lemon juice, sugar, honey and water, sometimes flavoured with musk and ambergris, and often cooled with ice or snow. A simpler *sherbet* was made of honey, or sugar, and water alone.

THE DISTRIBUTION OF IZNIK AND KÜTAHYA WARES IN THE PROVINCES

The pottery from Iznik and Kütahya was the result of improved technology and was apparently specifically designed for the tables of the upper and middle classes. The glossy white surface of this pottery, painted with metallic oxides, not only gave a colourful decoration, but also proved easily adaptable to meet new design-trends in the most fashionable Renaissance and Islamic styles of the time. Although tin-glazed pottery was a relatively expensive up-market product (tin had to be imported from abroad and was not cheap), these wares were always made primarily for daily use. In 1633 Evliya Çelebi describes a parade of 300 merchants of pottery before Sultan Murad IV. According to the Ottoman traveller the merchants adorned their shops with 'fayence of Nicaea (Iznik) and Kutahie'. Also interesting in this respect is Evliya's remark about the 20 'menders of broken cups' (Finjian Kindejian), who paraded before the Sultan while mending broken cups. This suggests there was even an industry of recycling broken pottery (from Iznik and Kütahya?) during the seventeenth century.

The colourful tablewares from Iznik and Kütahya were immensely popular, not only at home but also abroad, thanks to the thriving trade between the Ottoman Empire and the West. Fragments have been dug up in excavations from Fustat (old Cairo) in Egypt to Waltham Abbey (Essex) in Britain. Iznik ware was sold by numerous retailers in Istanbul, where the Venetian and Genoese merchants had headquarters, and through Venice found its way into Germany and the North. In the Journal of Stephan Gerlach, secretary of the Austrian embassy to the Porte between 1573 and 1578, it is noted that his master, David Ungnad, had spent over 100 ducats on pottery vessels and 1,000 thalers on 'Nicaean tiles' for shipment via Venice. In addition, two other documents identify the trade of Kütahya vessels in the early eighteenth century from Istanbul to France and the Crimea.

Excavations and field surveys in Greece have revealed that Iznik and Kütahya ceramics were also known in this part of the Ottoman Empire. Although not abundant, pieces of pottery from Iznik and Kütahya have been found at Athens, at Skyros, at Thessaloniki, at Kalapodi in Lokris, and at two sites in Boeotia. In addition, fragments of bowls and dishes from Iznik and Kütahya were found in some sixteenth- to eighteenth-century rubbish pits at an excavation in the historical centre of Thebes. The presence and quality of these ceramics in the Theban waste pits appear to represent the discards of a well-to-do urban household which was able to import decorative table wares from Turkey (67, 69).

Apart from these excavated finds we also have the so-called bacini as a source of information for the spreading of Iznik and Kütahya pottery. Bacini is the Italian term for decorated bowls that were embedded in church façades in both Italy and Greece from the eleventh century. For Greece, the custom remained popular into Ottoman times. Bacini of this period were inlaid in the walls of several churches in Attica, near Chalkis on Evvia, on Mount Athos, and on the islands of Salamis and Hydra. The import of these new fashionable tin-glazed imports from Turkey, which played such a large part in the dining ritual at the court of the Sultan, gave new impetus to developments in local ceramics in the provinces, most notably perhaps the Greek imitations of Iznik ware.

CONCLUSION

If Cornelis Calkoen's lunch at the Topkapi Palace on Sunday 14 September 1727 is reconstructed, it is clear that his banquet was held at the Council Hall in the second court before his official audience with Sultan Ahmed III. The Dutch ambassador surely had to eat from a *sini*, sitting on a low couch covered with carpets. He must have eaten with the fingers from a communal dish. Rice and mutton were doubtless served in large communal dishes, made of porcelain or Iznik ware and they drank *sherbet* during the meal and coffee after dinner.

According to Calkoen's report to his principals in Amsterdam, he had to eat from a communal dish with only three fingers. This presumably happened with his right hand according to Islamic doctrine (although this was not mentioned specifically by Calkoen). The Islamic culinary laws also demanded that the diners did not use knives to cut their meat, but broke and ate it with their fingers. Furthermore, all the guests were forced to eat in a hurry. White, freshly baked bread was laid on the *sini* for each diner, but there were no individual plates or napkins. The only utensils used were spoons, often beautifully made of ivory or ebony, for eating soup and compote. Calkoen and his fellow-diners had to follow the intricate etiquette of eating soup communally, whereby the right side of these spoons was used only to dish the liquid up and the left side to eat from it.

The dishes were handed over by court servants, forming a row from the palace kitchens (next to the Second Court) to the *sini* where Calkoen was eating. His lunch was probably prepared by approximately 600 professional cooks in the kitchens of the Sultan. On the menu were probably rice and mutton, and the food was served in large dishes, made of silver and expensive China porcelain. Perhaps the diners also ate from cheaper, everyday ware made at Iznik, although the heyday of this pottery centre was already over in the eighteenth century. After the lunch, the diners washed their hands and drank coffee. Perhaps this happened from decorative coffee cups, made at Kütahya, which were very popular among the Ottoman elite in the eighteenth century. In addition, the lemon *sherbet*, the only drink offered during the meal, could have been made in the imperial kitchens from lemons pressed with lemon squeezers, made at Kütahya. Both Iznik ware and Kütahya ware were the result of improved pottery technology and apparently specifically designed for the table of the Ottoman upper classes. It is, therefore, no coincidence that Cornelis Calkoen probably ate from an Iznik dish and certainly drank his coffee from a Kütahya cup.

Joanita Vroom

ACKNOWLEDGEMENTS

The following institution gave permission for reproduction of the paintings of Jean-Baptiste Vanmour: Rijksmuseum, Amsterdam (figs. *61, 63, 64, 65, colour plate 14*). All the paintings of Jean-Baptiste Vanmour were shown at an exhibition held in 2003 at the Rijksmuseum at Amsterdam and in 2004 at the Topkapi Palace in Istanbul. Photographs are by the author. The full title of Calkoen's description of his audience to the Ottoman court is `*R-elaes van het gepas-seerde in de publi-que audiëntien van zijne excellentie mijn-heere Cornelis Cal-koen, ambassadeur van wee-gens haer Hoog Mogende de Heeren Staatten Generael der Verenig-de Neederlanden bij zijn Sultanni-se Maje-stijt Achmet Ghan de derde van die naem*' ('Report of all things which happened during the public audience of his excellen-cy mister Cornelis Calkoen, ambassador of the splendid lords of the States General of the Dutch Republic at his Sultanic Majesty Achmed Khan III of that name". This docu-ment can be found in the Algemeen Rijksar-chief (The Hagu-e), Fami-lie-ar-chief Calkoen, 561.

BIBLIOGRAPHY

Abelmann, A. 'Cornelius Calkoen op audiëntie bij sultan Ahmed III' in H. Theunissen, A. Abelmann and W. Meulenkamp (eds), *Topkapi en turkomanie. Turks-Nederlandse ontmoetingen sinds 1600* (Amsterdam, 1989), pp.26-36

Akalin, S. 'Kütahya tiles and pottery in a historical perspective', in S. Akalin and H. Yilmaz (eds), *Delights of Kütahya* (Istanbul, 1997), pp.8-15

And, M., *Istanbul in the Sixteenth Century: the City, the Palace, Daily Life* (Istanbul, 1994)

Arsel, S. (ed.), *Timeless Tastes. Turkish Culinary Culture* (Istanbul, 1996)

Atasoy, N., and Raby, J., Iznik. *The Pottery of Ottoman Turkey* (London, 1989)

Bull, D., Renda, G. and Sint-Nicolaas, E., *The Ambassador, the Sultan and the Artist. An Audience in Istanbul* (Amsterdam/Zwolle, 2003)

Carswell, A.J., 'The lemon-squeezer. An unique form of Turkish pottery', *IVème Congrès International d'Art Turc* (Aix-en-Provence, 1971), pp.29-45

— , 'Kütahya tiles and ceramics', in M. Sadberk-Han (ed.), *Turkish Tiles and Ceramics* (Istanbul, 1991), pp.50-7

Dilger, K. *Untersuchungen zur Geschichte des Osmanischen Hoffzeremoniells im 15. und 16. Jahrhundert* (Munich, 1967)

Luttervelt, R. van *De 'Turkse' schilderijen van J.B. Vanmour en zijn school. De verzameling van Cornelius Calkoen, ambassadeur bij de Hoge Porte, 1725-1743* (Istanbul, 1958)

Mansel, P.H., *Constantinople. City of the World's Desire 1453-1924* (London, 1995)

Necipoglu, G., *Architecture, Ceremonial, and Power. The Topkapi Palace in the Fifteenth and Sixteenth Centuries* (London, 1991)

Reindl-Kiel, H. 'Die Lippen der Geliebten. Betrachtungen zur Geschichte der türkischen Küche', *Mitteilungen der Deutsch-Türkische Gesellschaft*, 116 (1993), pp.13-23

Rogers, J.M., 'Plate and its substitutes in Ottoman inventories', in M. Vickers (ed.), *Pots & Pans. A Colloquium on Precious Metals and Ceramics in the Muslim, Chinese and Graeco-Roman Worlds* (Oxford, 1986), pp.117-36

Savkay, T., 'The cultural and historic context of Turkish cuisine', in S. Arsel (ed.), *Timeless Tastes. Turkish Culinary Culture* (Istanbul, 1996), pp.75-88

Thiel, P.J.J. van *Alle schilderijen van het Rijksmuseum te Amsterdam. Volledig geïllustreerde catalogus* (Amsterdam/Haarlem, 1976), pp.741-50

Ursinus, M. 'Die Ess- und Trinkgewohnheiten der Osmanen', in *Türkische Kunst und Kultur aus osmanischer Zeit* (Recklinghausen, 1985) pp.155-58

Vroom, J., *After Antiquity. Ceramics and Society in the Aegean from circa the seventh to the twentieth centuries A.C. A Case Study from Boeotia, Central Greece* (Leiden, 2003)

— , 'Coffee and archaeology: a note on a Kütahya ware find in Boeotia, Greece', *Journal of the Netherlands Institute at Athens*, 4 (1996), pp.5-19

ten

EATING *AL FRESCO*: THE USE OF GARDEN BUILDINGS FOR DINING IN THE EIGHTEENTH-CENTURY ENGLISH PLEASURE GROUND

One of the most influential eighteenth-century commentators on the practice of gardening (then as now, a national obsession) was Thomas Whately. He first published his book *Observations on Modern Gardening* in 1770 and it subsequently ran to several reprints. On the subject of garden buildings he made the following observation:

> Buildings probably were first introduced into gardens merely for convenience, to afford refuge from a sudden shower, and shelter against the wind; or, to be seats for a party, or for retirement: they have now been converted into objects, and the original use is too often forgotten in the greater purposes to which they are applied; they are considered as objects only, the inside is totally neglected; and a pompous edifice frequently wants a room barely comfortable. Sometimes the pride of making a lavish display to a visitor, without any regard to the owner's enjoyments; and sometimes too scrupulous an attention to the style of the structure, occasions a poverty and dulness within, which deprives the buildings of part of their utility. But in a garden they ought to be considered both as beautiful objects, and as agreable retreats.

In general terms Whately may have been correct that there was a rise in the number of garden buildings that were constructed merely as shams, ornaments in the landscape with no useful purpose, but there is evidence to prove that during the 'long' eighteenth century (1700 – 1820), even at the date at which Whately was writing and towards its conclusion, garden buildings still had a variety of different uses. The most important and most frequent use was for dining. Up and down the country the leisured and landed classes were enjoying a variety of teas, picnics, ices and grand dinners in their temples, towers, grottoes and follies.

There is something fundamental about the pleasure of dining *al fresco*. This enjoyment is timeless and stretches from at least ancient Rome to the present day. The desire is perhaps greatest in the people of northern Europe, like the British, who do not have a climate that allows this to happen frequently, so they grasp every opportunity when it presents itself. During the eighteenth century the experience of the Grand Tour further imbued this desire with first-hand memories for the English milordi of picnics in the Roman Campagna and more distant undertones of classical revels in grottoes. Furthermore these *al fresco* experiences were tinged with a more English element of rural festival. They often took place during the hay-making season, when upper-class families would be at their country seats and able to watch the 'rustics' at work in the fields, sometimes from their garden buildings while sipping lemonade, though occasionally while taking part in the harvest themselves.

Eating outside was part of every house party, weather permitting, and an *al fresco* dinner or picnic would form the highlight of a stay at a country house. It was a chance for the host to impress and entertain his guests. Whether it was in the building itself, or outside with the building forming the focal point, dining was also fundamental to the experience of being in the garden – particularly for the owner and his intimate friends and family. Occasionally though, the gates were thrown open and the audience was much wider, as we shall see. However, for an activity that was so common the evidence is very fragmentary and has to be gleaned from a variety of different sources: written accounts of tours and visits, inventories of the contents of garden buildings, pictorial sources and the architecture or remains of the buildings themselves. Perhaps surprisingly, it is the pictorial sources that are most rare. Whilst almost every activity that could take place in a fashionable garden of the time is seen, for example in the engravings of Jacques Rigaud of the early 1730s, there is no scene in which the figures are depicted eating. This may be because refreshment was such a fundamental part of the enjoyment of an owner and so essential to hospitality that is was not novel enough for many artists to show. Alternatively artists may not have been invited into the intimate gathering that was a dinner in a temple and amateur artists, if they were guests, would have been too busy enjoying themselves to get out their sketch book.

Banqueting Houses had existed in England during the sixteenth and seventeenth centuries, usually small pavilions erected on the leads of the house, as at Longleat (Wilts), or close to the mansion, as at Montacute (Somerset). However during the eighteenth century they reached their apogee, moving much further away from the house, becoming larger, more elaborate and self-sufficient and this went hand in hand with the rise of the taste for the landscape garden.

This chapter will discuss the variety of different buildings around which eating in the garden centred, looking at their architecture and relationship to kitchen facilities before proceeding to discuss how these buildings and the gardens around them were actually used, how eating was part of the experience of being in the garden and why, in spite of Whately's warning, it was so popular.

THE BUILDINGS

The fact that today garden buildings are frequently, and sometimes erroneously, called 'banqueting houses' as a catch-all term is revealing. Today few visitors to fine eighteenth-century landscape gardens such as Stowe (Bucks), Stourhead (Wilts) or Studley Royal (Yorks) see buildings in use, but they will frequently call an ornamental building a 'banqueting house' without any firm knowledge of its original use. This perhaps shows that a consciousness of their function survives in our collective memories. Some buildings were known from their conception as 'The Banqueting House' and were built for this primary purpose, such as the Banqueting House at Gibside (Co. Durham), built in the 1740s (*70*). Many others were built for this purpose but given different names. Meanwhile, other garden buildings were built for a variety of purposes, such as fishing, quiet study and contemplation or bathing in a cold bath, and these functions can be discerned from an analysis of their architecture, both internal and external, their contents, where they occasionally survive, or more usually from inventories and bills. At grand sites, like Studley Royal, there could be a number of buildings used for eating in. The so-called Banqueting House was originally probably conceived as an orangery, although this would not have precluded it from being used for dining. The Octagon Tower was also used for dining and a tea was periodically taken at a number of the other buildings.

Buildings designed for multiple uses were commonly tripartite in form, usually with a central room and a room in each side wing. This gave the building a pleasing balance from the outside and allowed room for other functions, perhaps including somewhere to withdraw, and sometimes a bedroom or a kitchen. The Banqueting House at Gibside provides a good example of this tripartite form. Here there was a central 'Great Room' and behind, though staggered a little back, were two anterooms – one of which would have served as a kitchen – and both of which were equipped with closets probably for storing all the accoutrements necessary for serving and consuming food and drink. From the west closet a ladder led up to the roof enabling the building also to act as a belvedere, or viewing platform, and visitor descriptions tell us that the building was also used for small concerts.

70 The Banqueting House at Gibside (Co. Durham) seen from the drive below. Note the tripartite arrangement of the projecting central bay and flanking bays housing closets and kitchen

71 The elaborate plasterwork of the main room at Horton Menagerie (Northants). The interior was carefully restored by the late Gervase Jackson-Stops, Architectural Advisor to the National Trust

Even where eating was not the principal reason for the existence of a building there was often a room that could be used for this purpose. At Horton (Northants), the Menagerie, constructed in the 1750s to a design by Thomas Wright, was built as an eye-catcher to be seen on the horizon from the house and a focal point for the private zoo to the rear. In a circular enclosure of about two acres behind the building Lord Halifax's collection of exotic animals, including a tiger, a bear, racoons and wart-hogs, was kept. The central pavilion of the eye-catcher (flanked by wing walls ending in two smaller pavilions) was used for refreshments when visitors went to see the curious creatures, either directly from the house, or as part of a circuit around the park. The central room was decorated with elaborate plasterwork and there was a kitchen in the basement below (71).

Another good example of a garden building whose primary purpose was not eating, but which was used for eating in the course of other entertainments, is the Fishing Room at Kedleston (Derbys) (72). The building was designed in 1772 by Robert Adam, and performed a number of functions. Set on the edge of the lake, the flanking wings are boathouses (again a tripartite arrangement). The lower floor of the central pavilion contains a cold bath, fed from a nearby spring, and the room above gave access to the water for fishing, with rods being dangled from the window. This room, like the main room of the Menagerie at Horton, is richly decorated with plasterwork framing still lifes of a variety of fish, niches for sculpture and a fireplace. A fireplace is often a good indication that a

72 The Fishing Room at Kedleston (Derbys) where the two flanking bays hide boat houses

building was intended to be used frequently in many weathers and probably into the evening when a chill may descend even during high summer.

One thing that appears to have been desirable (though not essential), and that gives us firm evidence that a building was used for dining in, is the presence of a kitchen. There were three principal ways of arranging a kitchen facility for a garden building: in a side wing (as at Gibside), in the cellar or undercroft (as at Horton), or close by but concealed by planting, like that belonging to the Chinese Pavilion at Woburn (Beds). Isolated kitchens have survived far worse, in general, than those in the main building itself and their existence can sometimes only be determined by archaeological investigation. Beyond these examples, it is clear that some buildings used for dining were never provided with a kitchen.

John Aislabie and his son and heir, William, who owned two extensive landscape gardens in Yorkshire at Studley Royal and Hackfall, seem to have preferred the arrangement of a kitchen close by. At Hackfall, which was an independent, self-contained pleasure ground with no primary residence, this was obviously a sensible approach. It was practical too at the gothick Octagon Tower at Studley, which was not only a long way from the house, but entailed a difficult journey, both for the diners who must have been ready for refreshment by the time they reached the tower if they had walked, and also for those bringing and preparing the food. The Octagon Tower, built in the 1730s, is set on the top of a precipitous drop (*73*). It is reached via a serpentine tunnel through the cliff to the platform on which the tower sits. The entrance to the tunnel appears, from the platform, to be one of a pair of rustic 'caves' flanking the tower. However, the other 'cave' (*74*) was in fact a rudimentary kitchen for the warming of food before it was served in the tower just a few paces away. The tower must have made an intimate setting for tea or dinner. The ground plan is quite small and we know from a delivery note of 1768 that at that date it was furnished with a set of '6 arm'd walnut chairs', implying a very small party indeed for such a grand estate.

At Hackfall, around eight miles away, Aislabie entertained at two very different buildings, in very different settings: the Fisher's Hall in the lower part of the garden and close to the beautiful River Ure, and Mowbray Point, perched up on the top of the cliff above. The tourist, William Bray, described them both in 1783, starting with Mowbray Point: 'The building which affords this prospect, appears from different parts of the walk to be a ruin, but has two neat rooms in it, where, or in Fisher's Hall, Mr Aislabie sometimes dined, or indulged his friends with the liberty of so doing, and for this purpose kitchens are built near'. While there are no standing remains of the kitchen for the Fisher's Hall, fig. 75 shows the close proximity of the kitchen for Mowbray Point, hidden in the trees and now sadly ruinous.

73 The Octagon Tower at Studley Royal (Yorks) seen from below

74 The cave-like kitchen next to the Octagon Tower, Studley Royal (Yorks)

Fisher's Hall, like the tower at Studley, was an octagonal building and would have seated perhaps six or eight people at most. In contrast the Duke of Bedford, at Woburn, clearly entertained in his garden on an appropriately ducal scale. Here on an island in the lake, the journey to which added an extra dimension to the novelty, there was, to quote Defoe and Richardson, 'a very elegant and light Chinese temple, large enough for thirty people to dine in; and in the adjoining woods is a kitchen, &c. for making ready the repasts his grace takes in the temple'. Clearly when feeding so many people, again at a great distance from the house, a kitchen was a necessary requirement.

Perhaps the best place today to get an idea of what these buildings looked like when used on a regular basis is the Ionic Temple at Rievaulx Terrace (Yorks) (76). The terrace, high above Ryedale, is a lengthy walk and a continuation of the terrace at Duncombe Park, along the valley near Helmsley. The Ionic Temple would have formed the culmination of an excursion from the main house at Duncombe. Here the room is set for dinner and while the furniture and tableware is not exactly that used when the building was constructed in the 1750s, it is an accurate recreation based on inventory evidence. The table is laid, almost expectantly, for eight guests, the ornate chimney piece is intact and the interior is vibrant and colourful still – the ceiling and coving still have the original murals painted by Giuseppe Borgnis. In the basement are two rooms where the servants would have prepared the food for the guests upstairs.

75 Mowbray Point at Hackfall (Yorkshire). The remains of the kitchen building can be seen in the trees to the right of the view

THE EXPERIENCE

Undoubtedly different owners sought different things from their garden buildings. The capacity of the Chinese Temple at Woburn was unusual (and in scale rivalled perhaps only by the Temple of Concord and Victory at Stowe), and the table setting for the Ionic Temple at Rievaulx, which would hold a maximum of around 12 diners, was more typical. It is the intimate space that most garden buildings provided that is one of the keys to their popularity. Naturally a building must look attractive and form an interesting object in the landscape – as Whately acknowledged – but it should also justify its existence on a less superficial level. A fundamental part of the attraction of these buildings was the intimate spaces that they provided. The country house in the eighteenth century was a busy place and hospitality often expected rather than offered, moreover with many houses being improved or rebuilt entirely, the garden became a place to escape both the noise, and the dirt of building work as well as the throng of people, servants, hangers-on and guests who it was one's obligation rather than pleasure to host. The desire to escape such disruption sometimes led to unusual innovations, such as that at Holkham (Norfolk) where, while building work was in progress, food was taken out to be eaten in the garden by means of a specially adapted kind of barrow.

76 The interior of the Ionic Temple at Rievaulx Terrace (Yorks), set as if for a dinner

In a time when roads were still bad, though improving thanks to the turnpike network, guests might stay too long and be too numerous for an owner's taste. 'The Hospitality my Ancestors exercised for some generations at Croomb makes it impossible for me to effect any privacy or retirement there. It has always been an Inn and always must remain so', wrote Lord Coventry of his Worcestershire seat, Croome, in February 1750. It is no coincidence that the park is scattered with a variety of buildings from temples to simple alcove seats. Two buildings particularly afforded escape from the busy house: the Rotunda, close to the house in the home shrubbery, and the Temple Greenhouse in the pleasure ground some way off. By the 1760s the Rotunda was: 'fitted up as an evening apartment ... commanding not only charming views of the home scenery, but also of the distant and surrounding country'. As an 'evening apartment' quite close to the house it was the perfect place to stroll out to after dinner for dessert or coffee – which would, of course, be set up by the servants ready for one's arrival. The Temple Greenhouse, however, was the destination of more organised parties escaping the throng of the mansion. Its nominal function was as a home for tender, exotic plants including myrtles and geraniums. It was described as 'an extensive building, ornamented with statues of Pomona and Ceres at each end of the facade, and commanding a very fine view of the lake, bridge &c. This edifice is also used as a summer apartment'. The building was finished in 1763 to a design by Robert Adam. Original plans show that it was initially intended to have the typical tripartite arrangement, of three rooms of the type already discussed above. As well as being south facing, it was heated by a hypocaust (underfloor heating) so was always warm. The warmth and smell of the plants as well as the view it afforded across the park, must have made it the perfect place for picnics, teas or dinners and not just in high summer. This is acknowledged by the architecture and sculpture of the building. It is significant that it was not the goddess Flora who presides over this building but Ceres and Pomona, Roman goddesses of cereals and fruit respectively. It was still described as a 'lovely apartment' in 1824 by the Head Gardener, William Dean, in his description of the gardens.

Small outside apartments in which dinner was served to select groups of guests also necessitated fewer servants and encouraged less ceremony. During the eighteenth century dining in the house was a highly formal affair normally starting around four in the afternoon (though it became later as the century wore on and forms of artificial lighting improved) and continuing for several hours with many changes of course. The formality of British dining habits was remarked upon by continental visitors. François de La Rouchfoucauld, writing in the 1780s, observed that 'at four o'clock precisely you must present yourself in the drawing-room with a great deal more ceremony than we are used to in France ... you must be well-washed and well-groomed'. However the British, in their turn, also criticised their European neighbours. Lord Hervey's description of a dinner given by the Austrian envoy in London illustrates the extreme of extravagant, long-winded entertaining:

> thirty-eight dishes at a course, twelve removes, two courses and a dessert of arches, pyramids, giants, beasts, trophies etc., of barley sugar raised to such a tickish height that I believe it had been three weeks' building ... the dinner lasted three hours and half. The last two hours the doors were thrown open to the street and everybody that had curiosity to see and strength enough to push came into the rooms. Never was I so hot, so sick and tired in my life. All that dead flesh before and all that live flesh behind made the stench insupportable ... It was one of the most expensive, tawdry, ill understood, disagreeable pieces of German magnificence that was ever seen.

It is easy to see what was so attractive about dining with a small group of friends and family in intimate and comfortable surroundings with a beautiful view, with respite from the worst of the heat in the height of summer, and eating food produced on your own estate. It was part of the pleasure of being in the country. The fact that the fruit and vegetables would be grown in one's own kitchen garden, which one might inspect as part of a walk round the grounds, and that the meat might be from the sheep, cattle or deer grazing in the surrounding fields and parkland was important. Landowners took pride in both their livestock and their kitchen gardens, which as well as more conventional fruit could also produce exotics like melons and pineapples. Food in the country, where it was very fresh and in ready supply, was in stark contrast to that which was to be expected in London. Simon Varey has summed this up well:

> The pleasure of eating could certainly be the pleasure of somehow experiencing the country. Smollett's Matthew Bramble tends to idealise his life on a Welsh country estate, but really the point of his description of his food supply is that it is all fresh, natural and unadulterated. His cider and bread are home made; his claret 'of the best growth, imported for my own use, by a correspondent on whose integrity I can depend'; his sheep and calves (actually he refers to the animals as mutton and veal) raised on 'fragrant herbage' and 'the mother's milk' respectively.

At Wrest Park (Beds) the home of Jemima, Marchioness Grey, this was an acknowledged pleasure. Her sister-in-law Elizabeth Anson wrote in the 1740s, saying 'Papa has said so much at dinner today of Wrest, of the improvements made in the house, of the beauty of the garden, the excellence of the pineapples, cherries, strawberries, venison, etc., etc., and above all the company, that I can form no idea how it is possible to live anywhere else'.

Food eaten in one's garden building had to be simpler than that served at grand formal dinners, and this was even more necessary during a picnic. A building such as the Ionic Temple at Rievaulx just did not have the space for the 38 dishes at the Austrian envoy's dinner. There is also some evidence that the fine dinner services that developed during the century were not used either when dining away from the main house. At a picnic during a tour of the gardens at Esher, while he was at a house party there during the summer of 1763, Horace Walpole had a 'magnificent dinner, cloaked in the modesty of earthenware'. While they ate, 'French horns and hautboys' played on the lawn. Figure 77 is a rare view of an *al fresco* dinner at Mount Edgcumbe (near Plymouth, Devon) in the 1730s, by Thomas Badeslade, in which the party are entertained by a similar small band of musicians. Unfortunately, Walpole does not tell us what they ate. It is likely, though, that the food at Esher was cold. This would, by no means, have been unacceptable, especially at a picnic, and at Wroxton (Oxon), cold meats are mentioned as part of the experience of dining in the Chinese House in the garden. Ice creams were also enjoyed here. The first English ice cream recipes were published in 1718 by Mary Eales, confectioner to Queen Anne, and every great estate had an ice house to provided ice for both making the ice cream cold and keeping afterwards. Jane Austen, towards the end of the period, was

77 The Garden House and Wilderness at Mount Edgcumbe park (Devon) in 1735 by Thomas Badeslade

clearly familiar with the pleasures of eating cold food outside and her personal experiences were reflected in her novels. In *Sense and Sensibility*, first published in 1811, Sir John Middleton, a positive character, portrayed as a jolly, friendly and hospitable man, was 'in summer … for ever forming parties to eat cold ham and chicken out of doors'. The aborted trip to the fine estate of Whitwell, planned by Sir John, is described in anticipatory detail:

> The grounds were declared to be highly beautiful, and Sir John, who was particularly warm in their praise, might be allowed to be a tolerable judge, for he had formed parties to visit them, at least twice every summer for the last ten years. They contained a noble piece of water; a sail on which was to form a great part of the morning's amusement; cold provisions were to be taken, open carriages only employed, and everything conducted in the usual style of a complete party of pleasure.

The view by the landscaper Humphry Repton, of the scene at Prospect Hill, in the park of Longleat, published in his *Fragments* seven years after *Sense and Sensibility*, gives the impression of what this 'party of pleasure' might have looked like when settling down to eat and enjoy the view (*colour plate 16*).

If dinner lasted around three hours there would be time, in summer, for a stroll in the gardens before dark. This gave the opportunity of serving dessert (perhaps ice cream) or coffee at another location. After a dinner in the grotto at Stowe, Horace Walpole, that perennial party-goer, described how the diners walked to the Doric Arch which had been erected in honour of Princess Amelia, one of the guests. This was not a building which could hold a party of people being merely an arch, but with its setting in a grove of oranges, was a suitable focal point for coffee. Tea was perhaps a more frequently consumed beverage in the garden and no inventory of the contents of a garden building is complete without mention of the necessary equipment for making and serving it. In the closet of the Bowling Green House at Wrest Park there were:

> Two Corner Cupboards with Indian Pictures, A Mahogany Stand for a Tea Kettle, A Brass Lamp, Six Green Garden Chairs … A brass Tinder Box. In one of the Corner Cupboards – A colour'd China Tea Pot and Stand, A brown Tea Pot & colour'd Stand, Twelve colour'd Saucers, Nine Tea Cups Ditto, Eight Coffee Cups Ditto, Two Slop Basons Ditto, A Sugar Dish and Cover Ditto, A Milk Porringer Ditto, A Spoon Boat Ditto, One half pint Mugg Ditto, One blue & White Ditto, Six gilt Silver Tea Spoons in Shagreen Case.

The note for the delivery of various goods to Studley Royal tells us that the contents of 'Venus's Temple little Kitchen' included 'a Dozn of Chinese Cups & Saucers' and a 'Large Tea Pot' and in the Temple of Piety 'a Tea Table & a little Stand'. Perhaps one of the best known views of a party taking refreshment in the garden is the painting from 1762 by Johann Zoffany of the actor David Garrick and his wife, taking tea in their garden by the Thames at Hampton (Middlesex). A solitary servant is handing tea to Mrs. Garrick, and the couple sit accompanied by a guest at a simple table with dogs at their feet, while another guest fishes in the river. It is a scene of calm and relaxation.

Walpole's picnic at Esher took place after a tour of the grounds. This was typical, whether it was at the end or the start of a visit, the garden building and whatever refreshment was served in it, or at it, formed an essential part of the outing. At Rievaulx refreshment at the Ionic Temple would have formed the culmination of a visit from the house at Duncombe. After a drive along the terrace, during which the guests would have enjoyed the spectacular sight of the steep-sided valley with the river at the bottom building to the crescendo of the breath-taking view of the ruins of Rievaulx Abbey, they would then arrive at the Temple. In contrast to the experience to be had at Rievaulx, where refreshment was the culmination of the trip, Mowbray Point where food was served at Hackfall, was the first building to be visited as part of the tour. Here,

William Aislabie would take his guests in carriages from the main residence at Studley. They approached across a flat area and entered the building from the rear, then to shock and delight his guests he would open the shutters to reveal the vertical drop below the far side of the building and guests would realise, hopefully with exhilaration, that they were to dine on the top of a precipice. After refreshment was served, probably something fairly substantial since there was a kitchen hidden close by, a tour of the grounds would begin. The garden at Hackfall is situated in a steep valley and any walk to the bottom would involve a strenuous hike back up to Mowbray Point and the carriages, which would then have necessitated more refreshments at the end of the tour. The trick of balancing a building on the edge of a cliff for greater effect had already been used at Studley, though the effect was perfected at Hackfall – we should not underestimate the power of dramatic landscape to impress and excite the men and women of the eighteenth century. A generation earlier, John Aislabie had performed a similar trick when he sited the Octagon Tower. Here visitors would have climbed the hill through the tunnel and entered the back of the tower, and only when inside would they see that they were dining on the crest of a veritable precipice. The effect was the same at numerous sites. The Banqueting House at Gibside was entered via a loggia at the rear with the steep slope to the fore, and the Banqueting House at Hardwick (Co. Durham) and the belvedere at Bilham (Yorks) both exhibited similar characteristics.

Much has been said above of the virtues of the garden building for intimate private entertaining and in this, as well as for many other motives, there were plenty of opportunities for showing off one's grounds to the best advantage, though the audience was a small one. However, for many reasons – from impressing one's contemporaries and inferiors through to paternal beneficence and duty as the most influential figure in the locality – temples, towers and banqueting rooms were also the perfect focal point for public entertainments, feasts and fêtes. The grotto at Stowe (78) has already been mentioned in passing as the site of small parties, and indeed it does seem to have been the favoured spot for such junkets for at least two generations – even though the rich and powerful Temple-Grenville family could choose at least six other substantial buildings in the garden which would have been suitable. It was perhaps its setting, in a gentle, but narrow valley, embosomed by trees (in which to hang lanterns) and at the head of a lake, which was large enough for boats (for additional illuminations and to seat musicians) but small enough to ensure they did not drift away, that made it so perfect. As well as those private parties, which must have been enchanting, the family used it as the centre of larger entertainments for which the gates of the garden were flung open for all the respectable people of Buckingham to attend. William Bray described one such occasion in 1778: 'at the other end is

78 The grotto at Stowe (Bucks), scene of many *al fresco* dinners and fêtes

a Grotto, faced with flints and pebbles, in which Lord [Earl] Temple sometimes sups. On such occasions this grove is illuminated with a great number of lamps; and his Lordship with a benevolence which does him honour, permits the neighbourhood to share the pleasure of the evening with him and his company; the park gates being thrown open'. Allowing the public to watch one dine in one's grotto must have been a far more comfortable experience than that endured at the Austrian envoy's dinner by Lord Hervey.

The ultimate honour to one's house and garden, and the best excuse for such general hospitality, was a royal visit. In 1805, the Prince of Wales visited Stowe and was entertained by Earl Temple's nephew and heir, the Marquis of Buckingham. One of the guests was Betsey Fremantle, an intimate of the young ladies of the family, but not from quite such a high rung on the social ladder. Her description of the event shows that there were many things in common with the entertainment given twenty years before and for its detail is worth quoting at length:

> Dined at six & soon after nine, the Grotto being illuminated & the greatest concourse of people being assembled in the gardens, we all followed the Prince in Procession to the Grotto, among shouts of the multitude, who crowded so much upon us we had some difficulty in reaching the destined spot, which had the appearance of enchantment, the Grotto & surrounding scene being illuminated most brilliantly … the crowd was so

great, there being at least 10,000 people present that I remained in the Grotto, with Mrs. Berkeley, while the rest of the party walked round the water. On the Princes return to the Grotto, the Fire works commenced & succeeded wonderfully well, the water rockets had a particularly good effect & the whole went of with great eclat. I sat snug in the grotto by Charles Fox & had a good view of the whole. The Prince & Grandees, such as the Dutchess of Grafton, Ly Euston &c. supped in the Grotto, the Knyvetts sung Catches & Glees during supper. I went to one of the marquees, & did not get home till one o'clock.

CONCLUSION

Thomas Whately's complaint that towards the end of the eighteenth century fewer garden buildings were built to be used and that they were becoming merely 'objects' frequently wanting 'a room barely comfortable' may have reflected a general trend towards the building of sham castles, towers and ruins, but architectural history has not been the subject of this chapter and first hand descriptions, illustrations, inventories and the buildings themselves tell us a different story. The garden building was alive and well as a place of retreat, resort and entertainment and the consumption of food and drink was an integral part of these experiences. Moreover, the descriptions of the entertainments at Stowe, where the grotto played a central role, tell us something of the perceived status of the garden building. It is significant that the Prince of Wales, Duchess of Grafton and others of the highest social order were the ones who 'supped in the Grotto' while Betsey Fremantle went to one of the marquees for her supper. This impression is emphatically reinforced by a description of a 'breakfast' given by Georgiana, Duchess of Devonshire at Chiswick House, to celebrate her daughter's entrance into society in 1800. Lady Jerningham had been a guest, though much like Betsey Fremantle, not of the first importance and she wrote to her daughter telling of the party:

I am returned living from the Breakfast, I found it extremely pleasant and was very much amused. We got there a little after Three, and were told the Duchess was in the Pleasure Ground. We accordingly found her sitting with Mrs. Fitzherbert by an urn. Several Bands of Musick were very well placed in the garden, so that as soon as you were out of the hearing of one Band, you began to catch the notes of another; thus Harmony always met your ears. This sort of continued concert had always a pleasant effect upon my nerves. There is a Temple which was destin'd to be the Prince's Entertainment and was very prettily decorated with flowers. There were about 20 covers, and when we understood that the Duchess and these fine People were in the

Temple, we Goths took possession of the House, where we found in every room a table spread, with cold meat, fruit, ice, and all sorts of Wine. It is a fine House, and there are the most delightful pictures in it. After the eating and quaffing was over, the young ladies danced on the Green...

Whately surely had nothing to fear.

Kate Felus

ACKNOWLEDGEMENTS

For their encouragement and help the author would like to thank Andrew Barber and National Trust staff at Kedleston, Harry Beamish, Steve Desmond, Jon Edgar, Tim Knox, Oliver Jessop, Tim Mowl, Mark Newman, Tom Oliver, Nick Owen, John Phibbs and James Collett-White. Ian Berry and Mount Edgcumbe House and Country Park must also be thanked for their kind permission to reproduce the Badeslade view of the Garden House. *Colour plate 16* is reproduced by permission of the British Library, and fig. *71* was photographed by Tim Mowl. All other photographs are by the author.

BIBLIOGRAPHY

Batey, M. and Lambert, D., *The English Garden Tour* (London, 1990)

Bayne Powell, R., *Housekeeping in the Eighteenth Century* (London, 1956)

Bray, W., *Sketch of a Tour into Derbyshire and Yorkshire* (London, 1783)

Egerton Castle (ed.), *Jerningham Letters 1780-1843* (London, 1896)

Godber, J., *The Marchioness Grey of Wrest Park* (Bedford 1968)

Glanville, P. and Young, H. (eds), *Elegant Eating* (London 2002)

Headley, G. and Meulenkamp, W., *Follies* (London 1990)

Lewis, W.S. (ed.), *The Yale Edition of Horace Walpole's Correspondence* (New Haven, 1937-1961)

Strong, R., *The Artist and the Garden* (New Haven, 2000)

Varey, S., 'The Pleasures of the Table', in R. Porter and M. Mulvey Roberts (eds), *Pleasure in the Eighteenth Century* (London, 1996)

Whately, T, *Observations on Modern Gardening* (Dublin, 1770)

Wynne, E. (ed.), *The Wynne Diaries* (Oxford, 1935-1940)

INDEX

Aardenburg (Netherlands) 71

Abric Romaní (Spain) 12

Acton Court (Avon) 134

Acton Hall (Suffolk) 19

Adam, Robert 168, 174

Æthelthryth, St 17

Agde, council of 17

Ahmed III, sultan 145-7, 151, 159

Aislabie, John 169, 178

Aislabie, William 169

Alice de Bryene 19

Alpohonsi, Petrus 19, 87

Amelia, princess 177

Anne, queen 175

Anson, Elizabeth 175

Amsterdam (Netherlands) 145

Antioch (Syria) 33

Antwerp (Belgium) 79

Apollinaris, Sidonius 35

Aquae Helveticae 39-47

Arlon (Belgium) 26

Arthur, king 107

Arthur, Prince of Wales 126

Ashurbanipal, king 13

Athens 158

Augusta, princess 20

Austen, Jane 175-6

Aventinus, Lucius Secundinius 29

Babees Book 19

Baden (Switzerland) 39-47

Badeslade, Thomas 175

Bayeux Tapestry 91

Beatrice of Ornacieux 116

Beauvais (France) 94

Bedford, Duke of 171

Beowulf 16

Bergen (Norway) 68

Bergen-op-Zoom (Netherlands) 71

Berwick upon Tweed (Northumb) 124, 126

Bicorp (Spain) 12

Biebel, Elizabeth 104

Bilham 178

Bonn (Germany) 26

Borgnis, Giuseppe 171

Boscoreale (Italy) 31

Boué, Ami 156

Bowes, Sir Jerome 130

Bray, William 169, 178

Breda (Netherlands) 71

Brown, Marjorie 16

Bruges (Belgium) 68, 71, 82

Buckingham, Marquis of 179

Bynum, Caroline Walker 116

Calais (France) 106

Calkoen, Cornelis 143-8, 159-60

Camber Castle (Sussex) 134

Cambridge 108

Camille, Michael 117

Canterbury (Kent) 134

Carlin, Martha 18-19

Castiglione, Baldassare 19

Çelebi, Evliya 158

Celsus, Albucius 52

Chambers, Sir William 20

Charles VI, king 104, 111

Chelmsford 134

Chiswick House (Essex) 180

Chrystede, Henry 106

Cicero 35

Clark, Elaine 101

Claudius, emperor 34

Claudius 34

Cologne (Germany) 17, 26, 32, 78

Columbanus, St 16

Concilium Constantiense 19

Constance (Germany) 19

Copenhagen 79

Corning Museum of Glass 131

Corteziania 19

Count de Foix 106

Coventry, Lord 173

Cracow (Poland) 12

Croome (Worcs) 173

Culex 63

Danzig (Poland) 68

Dean, William 174

De Civilitate Morum Puerilum 19

de Honnecourt, Villard 108

de la Brocquière, Betrandon 149

de La Rouchfoucauld, François 174

de Lysle, Anthony 130

Defoe, Daniel 171

Degrevant, Sir 108

Delft (Netherlands) 71

Denis, St 111

Derby, Earl of 105

di Angelo dal Gallo, Vincenzo 130

Diogenes the Cynic 35

Dives 111

Disciplina Clericalis 19

Dordrecht (Netherlands) 71

Douceline of Marseilles 116

Dresden (Germany) 153

Drinkwater, John 30

Dublin 106

Duke de Berry 112

Duke of Gloucester 106

Duke of Northumberland 122

Dunbabin, Katherine 14, 50, 55-6

Duncombe Park 171, 177

Dyer, Christopher 102

Eales, Mary 175

Edward III, king 95

Edward IV, king 95

Edward, the Black Prince 107

Effros, Bonnie 17

Elblag (Poland) 79

Elizabeth I, queen 120-2, 124, 138

Epigrams 35

Erasmus of Rotterdam 19

Esher 177

Etruria (Italy) 14

Exeter 108

Fasti 58

Fragments 176

Fremantle, Betsey 179-80

Froissart, Jean 107

Fustat (Egypt) 158

Gaimster, David 18

Garrick, David 177

Gawain, Sir 107

Geography 35

George, St 111

Georgiana, Duchess of Devonshire 180

Gerlach, Stephan 158

Gibraltar 11

Gibside 165, 169, 178

Glimmingehus (Sweden) 78-9

Grafton, Duchess of 180

Green Knight 107

Greenwich 122

Gregory of Tours 17, 28

Greifswald (Germany) 76, 79

Grenal, Richard 138

Grey, Marchioness Jemima 175

Grosseteste, Bishop of Lincoln 102

Guildford (Surrey) 111

Guy of Warwick 112

Haapsalu (Estonia) 73

Haci Hürrem Bey 156

Hackfall (Yorks) 169, 177-8

Hadrian's villa (Italy) 52

Halifax, Lord 168

Hampton (Middlesex) 177

Hardwick Hall (Derbys) 112

Harris, Sir Christopher 124

Harrison, William 121-2, 129, 141

Heal, Felicity 108

Helgersen, Jens 79

Helmsley 171

Henisch, Bridget Ann 107

Henry III, king 104, 111

Henry V, king 111

Henry VI, king 111

Henry VIII, king 123

Herculaneum (Italy) 49

Hervey, Lord 174, 179

Historia Augusta 35

Histories 34, 39

Holkham 172

Homer 13

Horaces 33

Horton (Northants) 168-9

Igel (Germany) 29, 32

Iliad 13

Isabella, queen 104, 113

Isola Sacra (Italy) 59-63

Issoire, bishop 17

Istanbul 143-61

Iznik (Turkey) 153-56, 158, 160

Jane Mary of Maillé 116

Jashemski, Wilhelmina 49, 57

Jerningham, Lady 180

Jerusalem 111

Jesus 107

John II, king 107

John atte Forth 111

Judith 16

Julius Caesar 15

Juvenal 35

Kalapodi (Greece) 158

Kalmar (Sweden) 74, 79

Kedleston (Derbys) 168

Kempe, Margery 116

Kew (Surrey) 20

Kings Lynn (Norfolk) 116

Kołobzreg (Poland) 72

Knight of the Tour-Landry 109

Knossos (Crete) 13

Krapperup (Sweden) 78-9

Kronoberg (Sweden) 79

Kütahya (Turkey) 155-9

Kuusisto (Finland) 76

L'Art de Bien Traiter 128

Langerwehe (Germany) 74

Langland, William 18, 115

Langres (Italy) 58

Launceston Castle (Cornwall) 96

Lazarus 111

Leiden (Netherlands) 71

Letters 52

Life of the Roman People 49

Lihula (Estonia) 72-73

Lincoln 102

Lindholmen (Denmark) 78

London 18-19, 68, 74, 82-3, 123-4, 126, 130-1,
    137, 140, 174

Longleat (Wilts) 164, 176

Louis IX, king 107

Lübeck (Germany) 68, 71

Lucius Verus 35

Ludgershall (Wilts) 111

Lund (Sweden) 79

Lüneburg (Germany) 79

Luttrell, Geoffrey 117

Luttrell Psalter 117

Mainz (Germany) 26

Malaga (Spain) 78

Malmö (Sweden) 79

Malmöhus (Denmark) 78

Mannyng, Robert 115

Marshall, Earl 105

Martial 35

Martial, St 107

Maternus, Gaius Iulius 26

Maurentania (Africa) 30

Mehmed II, sultan 149

Montacute (Somerset) 164

Montagu, Lady Mary Wortley 156

Mount Edgcumbe (Devon) 175

Murad II, sultan 149

Murad IV, sultan 158

Murena 35

Nakht, noble 12

Natural History 31, 35

Neumagen (Germany) 26

Nicaea (Turkey) 158

Ninevah (Assyria) 13

Nonsuch Palace (Surrey) 134

Northampton 111

Northumberland 122

Novgorod (Russia) 18, 68, 80, 81-2

Nuremberg (Germany) 18

Observations on Modern Gardening 163

On Farming 56

Odyssey 13

Orfeo, Sir 108

Ostia (Italy) 52, 59, 63

Ovid 58

Oxford 134

Paestum (Italy) 14

Paris 18, 104

Pärnu (Estonia) 73

Peking 153

Percy, Henry 122

Petronius 32-3, 35, 51, 62

Pevensey (Sussex) 91

Piers the Plowman 18

Platt, Colin 98

Platter, Thomas 123-6, 140

Pliny the Elder 31, 35

Pliny the Younger 52

Pompeii (Italy) 31, 49, 52-3, 55-7, 59, 62

Postel, Guillaume 150

Prince of Wales 179-80

Prittlewell (Essex) 16

Pskov (Russia) 81

Purcell, Nicholas 57

Raeren (Belgium) 74, 94

Rembrandt, painter 145

Repton, Humphry 176

Réville (France) 17

Richard II, king 105

Richardson, Samuel 171

Riga (Latvia) 68, 78

Rigaud, Jacques 164

Rievaulx Terrace (Yorks) 171, 177

Rome 15, 34, 59

Rostock (Germany) 79

Rostock-Stralsund (Germany) 68

Rouen (France) 88

Roztoky (Czech Republic) 12

Saintonge (France) 91-4

Satires 33, 35

Saturninus, Gnaeus Vibrius 59, 62

Satyricon 32-3, 35, 51, 62

Scarborough (Yorks) 112

Securus, Lucius Secundinius 29

Sense and Sensibility 176

Sheffield Manor (Yorks) 134

Siegburg (Germany) 74, 76

Six, Jan 145

Skanör (Denmark) 73

Skyros (Greece) 158

Southampton (Hants) 87-91, 93-7, 131, 137

Spencer's Farm (Berks) 96

Sponsler, Claire 116

Stockholm 74, 75, 79

Stow, John 123, 140

Stowe (Bucks) 165, 172, 177-8

Strabo 35

Studley Royal (Yorks) 165, 169-71, 177

Suetonius 34

Suleyman the Magnificent 149-50

Swabey, ffiona 19

Tacitus 34, 39

Tallinn (Estonia) 73, 74, 76

Tartu (Estonia) 73, 76

Temple, Earl 179

The Battle of Maldon 16

The Hague 145

Thessaloniki (Greece) 158

Tiberius, emperor 52

Topkapi Palace (Istanbul) 143, 145-8, 151-4, 159

Training for a Gentleman 87

Trier (Germany) 26

Tubero, Quintus 35

Turku (Finland) 74, 75

Ungnad, David 158

Unton, Sir Henry 128

Utrecht (Netherlands) 71

Vanmour, Jean-Baptiste 145-7

van Zeggelen, M.C. 145

Varey, Simon 175

Varro 49, 56

Venice 130

Verzelini, Giacomo 130

Vindonissa (Switzerland) 39, 44

Virgil 63

von Wedel, Lupold 122-26, 140

Waldenburg (Germany) 74

Walpole, Horace 175, 177

Waltham Abbey (Essex) 158

Whately, Thomas 164, 165, 172, 180

Wilfrid, St 17

William the Conqueror 91

Willis, Steve 36

Winchester (Hants) 96

Woburn (Beds) 169, 171–2

Wratislaw, Baron Wenceslas 151

Wrest Park (Beds) 175, 177

Wright, Thomas 168

Wroughton Copse (Wilts) 96

Wroxton (Oxon) 175

Yeavering (Northumb) 16

Zoffany, Johann 177

If you are interested in purchasing other books published by Tempus,
or in case you have difficulty finding any Tempus books in your local bookshop,
you can also place orders directly through our website

www.tempus-publishing.com